To Granny,

with kisses and hugs
From the author

Jack

ps35

HIDDEN TREASURES

SOMERSET

Edited by Kelly Oliver

First published in Great Britain in 2002 by
YOUNG WRITERS
Remus House,
Coltsfoot Drive,
Peterborough, PE2 9JX
Telephone (01733) 890066

HB ISBN 0 75432 867 8
SB ISBN 0 75432 868 6

FOREWORD

This year, the Young Writers' Hidden Treasures competition proudly presents a showcase of the best poetic talent from over 72,000 up-and-coming writers nationwide.

Young Writers was established in 1991 and we are still successful, even in today's technologically-led world, in promoting and encouraging the reading and writing of poetry.

The thought, effort, imagination and hard work put into each poem impressed us all, and once again, the task of selecting poems was a difficult one, but nevertheless, an enjoyable experience.

We hope you are as pleased as we are with the final selection and that you and your family continue to be entertained with *Hidden Treasures Somerset* for many years to come.

CONTENTS

All Saints CE Primary School
                Jane Allen   1

Ashcott CP School
                Alice Edmunds   1
                Katherine Wright   2
                Fiona Hill   2
                Ellie Chilcott   2
                Sally Stockman   3
                Aimee Wyatt   3
                Rebecca Wright   4
                Matilda Grainger   5
                Eddie Hill   6
                James Thompson   6

Horsington CE Primary School
                Paul Durant   7
                Matthew Jamieson   8
                Tom Rumbelow   8
                Joshua Farrant   8
                Jack Carnell   9
                Terry Thorne   9
                Annabel Stanford   10
                Amy Sanger   10
                Lauren Collins   10
                Joshua Barron   11
                Rachael Fox   11
                Hollie White   12
                Glen Warren   12

Huish Episcopi Primary School
                Katie Jameson   12
                Christine Brett   13
                Hollie Westlake   14
                Tom Spoors   14

Kelly Frome   15
Sophie Miller   16
Harriet Forster   16

Keinton Mandeville Primary School
          Amy Sweetman   17
          Alex Poyner   17
          Tonya Greenidge   18
          Thomas Cella   18
          Inina Opstrup   19

Kewstoke Primary School
          Tiffany Trewin   19

Long Sutton Primary School
          Jed Collis   20
          Catalina Moffat   20
          James Kew   21
          Jane Rieveley   21
          Matthew Cardwell   21
          Nathan Norris   22
          Stephen Wall   22
          Adrian Dyer   22
          Georgina Phillips   23
          Tom Jones   23
          Oliver Dent   23
          Abigail Smith   24
          Charlotte Hole   24
          Isabel Ronchi   24
          Amy Wicks   25
          Lydia Cox   25
          Amy Collins   25
          John Barlow   26
          Matthew Keech   26

Millfield Prep School
          Luke Ward   26
          Grace Hills   27

Beatrice Wood	27
Lily Parkinson	28
Alexandra Franklin	28
Felicity Whitehouse	28
Holly Aungiers	29
Tiphanie Bintcliffe	29
Christie Jones	30
Hugh Wyatt	30
Henry Fabre	31
Zoe Wall	31
Max Adams	32
Daniel Lewis-Williams	32
Harry West-Taylor	33
Piers Denning	33
Lucy Etherington	34
Megan Hill	34
Sarah Woods	35
Jack McNeil	35
Toby Lett	36
William Heywood	36
Elisabeth Foulkes	37
Tom Moore	38
David Littman	38
Alastair Wall	39
Chloë Warren	39
Charlie Martin	40
Edmund Rhind-Tutt	40
Clare Haskins	40
Emma Johnson	41
Richard Gabb	41
Shakira Cropper	41
Laura Coates	42
Victoria Berryman	42
Christopher Deakin	43
Charlotte Barraclough	43
Keith Showering	44

Redstart Primary School

Megan Manley	44
Jessica Simpson	45
Joshua Kilbride	46
Stephanie Wells-Burr	46
Kathryn Hunt	47
Kerrie Winter	47
Alastair Haste	48
Kayleigh Vaux	48
Nathan Skyrme	48
Jade Dunning	49
Karl Fletcher	49
Rachel Cox	50
Marsha Hall	50
Megan Butt	51
Sophie Harris	51
Esther Brown	52
Abbie Bide	52
Sarah Bishop	52
Joanna Dymel	53
Emilee Glenn	53
Robert Gibbs	53
Samantha Curnock	54
Megan Emery	55

St Aldhelm's CE Primary School, Doulting

Louisa Mair	55
Charlotte Mair	56
Cianni Brook	56
Lauren Luxford	57
Michael Barnett	57
Sarah Ford	58
Sam Moulton	58
Bethany Manders	59
Suzy Corner	60
Katie Burr	60
Nathan Young	61
Kathryn Cawsey	61

Louisa Garbett	62
Esme Stevens	62
James Ford	63
Millie Ayton-Moon	63
Fiona Stevens	64
Jack Vaughan	64
Jessica Wilkins	65

St Joseph's RC Primary School, Burnham-on-Sea

Joseph Niblett	65
Hayley Mear	66
Millie Taylor	66
Siân Priory	67
Briony Cooper	67
William Tasker	68
Rebecca Pearce	68
Ellie Fry	69
Anna Beck	69
Gregory Guyatt	70
Caine Draper	70
Katherine Mckenzie	71
Natasha Allen	71
Emma Shattock	72

Sedgemoor Manor Junior School

Dean Goldsmith	72
Katie Lock	73
Abigail Brennan	73
Mercedes Bowers	74
Danny Hemmings	74
Tayia Jade Hiroz	75
Adam Benner	76
Andrew Griffiths	76
Reece Standerwick	76
Kimberley Thomas	77
Nick Phillips	77
Adam Busby	78
Jodie Williams	78

Emily Ives	79
Joshua Baker	79
Conner Hillman	80
Becky Rowley	80
Holly Miller	81
Christopher Thomas	81
Zoe Harris	82
Kyle Frost	82
Rachel Selway	83
Dominic Best	83
Jennifer Prowse	84
Lauren Howe	84
Kirsty Newman	85
Ryan Daly	85
Jodie Searle	86
Natasha Baker	86
Jade Williams	87
Ashley Rawles	87
Larissa Turner	88
Leanne Marie Hale	88
Gemma Wood	89
Charlie Oram	90
Abby Mitchell	90
Marcus Bell	91
Paige Stacey	92
Christopher Winn	92
Holly Ingram	93
Kirsty James	93
Jasmine Lewis	94
Mena Hajar	94
T-Anna Buxton	95
Brett Collins	95
Matthew Williams	96
Gary Agnew	96
Jade Roberts	97
Hayley Moule	97
Lloyd Hooper	98
Stephen Cross	98

Sandra Boulton	99
Gavin Smith	99
Stacey Mirto	100
James Taylor	100
Mikki Hole	101
Ashley Mills	101
Rebecca Addicott	102
Marissa O'Neill	102
Stephanie Nichols	103
Ryan Millis	103
Mason Galloway	104
Jessica Woollan	104
Shelley Hooper	105
Jessica Bowers	106
Ashley Scott	106
Lewis Eichmann	107
Adam Howe	107
Ellie May	108
Sam Saunders	108
Sam Facey	109
Jayne Tucker	109
Stacey Hurley	110
Jamie Pike	110
Kirsty Hole	111
Liam Cornell	111
Sarah Hutt	112
Jodie Jodkowski	112
Liam Pope	113
Amy Leitch	113
Matthew Entwistle	114
Tanya Varnam	114
Andrew Rees Peacey	115
Chris Power	115
Marcus Keen	116
Ashley Addicott	116
Charlotte Constable	117
Lauren Huxtable	117
Rosie Keirle	118

Amber Baker	118
Dean Mills	118
Stephen Blake	119
Sarah Collins	119
Hannah Whitehouse	120
Joshua Godfrey	121
Susan Gardner	121
Nathan Mitchell	122
Kirsty Lilley	122
Sam Godfrey	123
Johno Speed	123
Damian Brown	124
Kirstin Trunks	124
Orion Draper	125
Kerry Mills	125
Jennifer Parsons	125
Ilkay Kolcak	126
Liam Riddle	126
Samantha Webber	126
Ben Ward	127
Joanna Hall	127
Tanya Hughes	128
Hannah Cobbin	128
Krystal Brennan	128
Shavana Ball	129
Lloyd Hooper	129
Lauren Griffiths	129
Jade Smith	130
Sadie Trent	130
Jenny Rowe	130
Jade Gillard	131
Becky Hopper	132
Carla Lambert	132
Rachel Fry	132
Jordan Hosey	133
Holly Keirle	133
Luke Hardwell	134
Kirstin White	135

Cassandra Gillard	136
Jemma Tomlinson	136
Cameron Taylor	137
Ben Patrick	137
Reece Galloway	138
Sophie Dilbo	138
Scott James	139
Rosemary Ingram	139
Sophie Withers	140
Kim Dibble	140
Natasha Puddy	141
Chloé Bowen	141
Jade Stone	142
Miles Beacham	143

West Coker Primary School

Richard Townsend	143
Gemma Louise Bowditch	144
Gemma Powell	144
Amy Harriss & Holly Dover	145
Adam Beckey	145
Sherrie Dampier & Emma Simpson	146
Robert Curtis, Terry Sollis	
& Katherine Foster	146
Joshua Nutland	147
Holly Edmonds	147
Katherine Foster	148
Earle Neville	149

Woolavington Village Primary School

Vicky Moore	149
Carrianne Smith	150
Holly Cox	150
Deborah Hirst	151
Liam Whatley	151
Ben Hiley	151
Iona Neilson	152
Michael Moares	152

Honey Halliday   152
Holly Jago   153
Tiffany Boobyer   153
Joanne Marsh   154
Stacy Moore   154
Ryan Dicks   155
James Olive   155
Gabrielle Roper   155
Dominik Griffin   156
Hannah Halliday   156
Vikki Thomas   157
Amy Sparrow   157
Cally Etherington   158
William Newcomb   158
Yasmin Millverton-Collier   159
Richard Stewart   159
Grace Dear   160

The Poems

MY TEDDY SPOKE

My teddy spoke the other day,
He said there was something interesting he had to say.
He spoke with a cheeky grin,
He said, 'I love you deep within.
I love you, yes I do,
I really hope you love me too.
I'm a super, handsome bear,
I have curly, shiny, green hair.
You are my best friend,
Our friendship will never end.'

Jane Allen (11)
All Saints CE Primary School

THE WAY THE WORLD MOVES AROUND ME

The hills are rolling away and away,
The seas are lapping over and over,
The trees are swaying side to side,
The birds are chirping sweetly and softly,
The dolphins jumping higher and higher,
The fishes swimming further and further,
The ducks swimming faster and faster,
The grass all green and getting longer and longer,
A hot air balloon going up and up,
The watches ticking on and on,
The torches shining brighter and brighter,
The horses galloping quicker and quicker,
My little baby sister crying more and more,
The lightning crashing louder and louder,
This is the way the world moves around me!

Alice Edmunds (8)
Ashcott CP School

MY SUPER GRAN

My gran is as pretty as a rose,
Her hair is like a wisp of a spider web,
Her eyes are like two sour lemons,
Her face is like squirty, spiral cream.
When she walks, she is like a calm turtle,
When she sits, she is like a silent harvest mouse,
When she laughs, she is like a giggly hyena,
When she sleeps, she is like a rolled-up hedgehog.
The best thing about my gran is,
She's the best gran in the world.

Katherine Wright (9)
Ashcott CP School

SQUIRREL

Squirrel,
Tail flashes by,
So silently he leaps.
In the dark and gloomy forest,
He hides.

Fiona Hill (11)
Ashcott CP School

TORTOISE

Sleeps in some leaves,
Hiding in the forest,
His polished shell on his back,
Quiet.

Ellie Chilcott (10)
Ashcott CP School

THE UNICORN

The unicorn is a shy creature,
If you see one don't spoil its feature,
Beautiful and sleek, quiet and meek.

When a man sees a unicorn he only sees a white mare,
The man will see a man of long, silvery-white hair,
But wait, what's that over there?
It must be a figure of my imagination,
It must be . . .

A unicorn's coat is silvery-white,
It's the most beautiful sight,
The best sight in the world has to be
A unicorn, you have to see.

Sally Stockman (11)
Ashcott CP School

THE ROBIN

In summer the skies are filled with song,
And now in winter the songs are gone.
But in my garden is an apple tree,
Where a single bird comes to sing for me.
Small crumbs are all that I have to pay,
For his cheerful song sung every day.
Warm and snug by my cosy fire,
I won't forget that solo flier.
And when summer swallows perch on the wire,
My friendly robin will lead his choir.

Aimee Wyatt (8)
Ashcott CP School

GIANTS' LAND

We didn't see giants
in giants' land,
but we saw
where the giants had been.

We saw where they had crushed
trees and houses
and people running everywhere.

We saw wet patches
where giants' sloppy spit
had disintegrated into nothing.

We saw giants' weapons
lying about,
so we dared not to go and touch them.

And draped from a branch,
we saw parts of a shirt,
dirty, smelly, worn out.

We didn't see giants
in giants' land,
but this was the closest
we'd ever been

to believing.

Rebecca Wright (11)
Ashcott CP School

TRICORN WOOD

We didn't see Tricorns
In Tricorn wood,
But we saw where
The Tricorns had been.

We saw deep, curved hoof prints
In soft green grass
Where a mythical creature had stood.

We saw great clumps
Of tree leaves missing, where
A Tricorn's teeth had been.

We saw big lumps of flowers
That had been trampled
And we saw little chips of horn
Which had been cut off,

And slouched over branches,
We saw tail hairs which
Had been caught and pulled off.

We didn't see Tricorns
In Tricorn wood,
But this is the closest
We'd ever been

To believing.

Matilda Grainger (11)
Ashcott CP School

MURDER AT MANOR HOUSE

There's going to be a murder . . .
Tonight at Manor House.
Just because I'm a mere servant,
I'm not short of a brain.

Up the winding stairs,
Going round in my head, who is the murderer?
But who will be the victim?
These are the questions.

Both the children asleep, their mother asleep too.
The curtain flaps, like someone's climbed in
And the wind howls.
But wait, where is the master?

Along the creaky corridor,
My poor bare feet feeling warm,
As if someone has walked before me,
Then down the winding stairs.

The shot of a gun!
A long sigh,
The last sigh of
J E Banks . . .

Eddie Hill (8)
Ashcott CP School

GUTS AND GORE

Guggle, guggle, guts and gore,
Everybody has a war.
Everybody fights to the death,
As you can tell, there is no ref.
After all there is no war,

There is nobody left to gore.
All the guts are everywhere,
There is nobody left to care.
Guggle, guggle, guts and gore,
That's the end of our bloody war!

James Thompson (10)
Ashcott CP School

TREASURE HUNT

I looked upstairs,
I looked downstairs,
I looked in the cellar,
I looked in the garden,
But I could not find the treasure.

I looked in my room,
I looked in the lounge,
I looked in the kitchen,
I looked in the bathroom,
But I could not find the treasure.

I asked my brother,
I asked my mother,
I asked my father
And he said,
'What's that in your pocket?'
'My treasure!' I yelled.

Paul Durant (9)
Horsington CE Primary School

HIDDEN TREASURE

Treasure, treasure, down below.
Where, in the sea below,
Or down a well?
I cannot tell!

Where is the treasure?
I do not know.
Well is it on a pirate ship?
I don't know where it is.
I'll ask my mother, she will know.

Matthew Jamieson (8)
Horsington CE Primary School

THE THINGS IN A TREASURE CHEST

A pirate's handkerchief covered with shiny jewels,
An old, dusty sailor's leg covered with dust
And white pieces of cloth,
A ruby-red necklace from a mermaid who
Lived in a dark black cave,
A letter from the greatest pirate in the seven seas, Mallgog,
An the best thing of all, a map to find the treasure,
But it's found!

Tom Rumbelow (8)
Horsington CE Primary School

HIDDEN TREASURE

Where is the treasure?
Is it here, is it there?
Is it in my garden,
Or under the stairs?

Where is the treasure?
I do not know!
Is it under my bed,
Or did I throw it in the bin?

Joshua Farrant (9)
Horsington CE Primary School

THE HIDDEN TREASURE

Once I was a pirate.
I found some hidden treasure.
We pulled it up,
We looked inside.
Inside was a golden kettle,
But it wasn't the right chest,
So we got a telescope
And saw the golden chest!

Jack Carnell (8)
Horsington CE Primary School

PRECIOUS THINGS

Golden treasure that sparkles in the moonlight,
A mean pirate with one wooden leg on the left,
Sparkling jewels on his precious handkerchief,
Golden treasure that sparkles underneath the light of the moon.
Dancing pirates on board the ship,
Pirates drinking cider on board,
Pirates asleep, quickly awake.

Terry Thorne (8)
Horsington CE Primary School

TEN THINGS FOUND IN A TREASURE CHEST

A pirate's leg, well worn,
A letter from Granny saying not to be late for tea,
A sailor's scarf covered in seaweed,
A beautifully decorated crown,
A skeleton of a sailor.

A bag of silver pennies,
A glittering necklace,
A swirling whirlpool,
A letter in a bottle,
A golden box covered in coloured glass,
These things are found in a treasure chest.

Annabel Stanford (8)
Horsington CE Primary School

SECRET TREASURE

Treasure hidden in the sea,
Nobody knows where it may be,
If it is here or there,
They look up,
They look down,
They do not know if it's in town.

Amy Sanger (7)
Horsington CE Primary School

THE TREASURE BOX

Where is the treasure?
Where is the treasure?
Where is it?
I need the treasure.

Are you in the sea?
Are you buried underground?
Are you anywhere?
Treasure, I need you!

Lauren Collins (8)
Horsington CE Primary School

TEN THINGS FOUND IN A TREASURE CHEST

A pirate's wooden leg,
The tattered flag of an old ship,
A golden candlestick, candle half burnt,
Half the head of a sailor,
A dented cannonball with its dented cannon,
The captain's sword bent in half,
The sailor's compass, the dial not working,
The captain's finger with a ring on it,
A dead guard dog,
A wicked grinning skull.

Joshua Barron (8)
Horsington CE Primary School

DEEP SEA TREASURE

Under the sea, dolphins swim,
Sea horses dance and swirl,
The sharks lurk beneath the coral,
Turtles swim gracefully along.
Under the deep sea lies treasure,
Open to find to your surprise,
A land of glistening jewels.

Rachael Fox (8)
Horsington CE Primary School

THE BURIED TREASURE CHEST

Where is the treasure, in the sea?
Where is the treasure, looking for me?
Where is the treasure, playing hide-and-seek?
So please treasure chest, come and find me.
I remember where I put the treasure,
In the garden.
Hooray, I've found it!

Hollie White (8)
Horsington CE Primary School

TREASURE

Where is the treasure?
Is it in the attic,
Or is it in the garden,
Or might it be in a lake,
Or might it just be my family?

Glen Warren (7)
Horsington CE Primary School

MY FAVOURITE BOOK

There are millions of books in the world,
Some people read them until the ends are curled,
But I just have one favourite book,
Come and see, have a good look.
I hope you'll enjoy it, I really do,
I hope you'll say yeah instead of boo.

Every night when I go to bed,
I read it until my head drops dead,
And then I wake in the morning,
Knowing night is far from dawning.
So that's my favourite book,
Come and see, have a good look.

Katie Jameson (10)
Huish Episcopi Primary School

IT WAS SO QUIET

It was so quiet that I heard
My heart singing,
Like a bird in harmony
Saying that dawn had broken.

It was so quiet that I heard
A silent raindrop fall from
The window like the spray
From a fireman's hose,
Acting like a snake, spitting its venom.

It was so quiet that I heard
A dragon burning its prey,
Like a barbecue blazing,
Like a belly dancer whooshing
Into the night sky.

It was so quiet that I heard
Bombs hitting houses,
Children running about
Acting like headless chickens
Pecking into the mouldy mud.

Christine Brett (10)
Huish Episcopi Primary School

ALONE

As I sat in the chair all alone,
I saw all the children playing,
While my mother made me clean the hay,
I had no one to tell or phone.

As I sat in the chair all alone,
I saw all the children going fishing
And oh, I was wishing,
I had no one to tell or phone.

As I sat in the chair all alone,
I saw all the children walking their dogs,
As they picked up a jog,
I had no one to tell or phone.

As I sat in the chair all alone,
I saw the girls dancing,
I would have been prancing,
I had no one to tell or phone.

As I sat in the chair all alone,
I saw all the children laughing and joking,
They were all poking,
I had no one to tell or phone.

Hollie Westlake (10)
Huish Episcopi Primary School

MY FRIEND FRASE

My friend is called Frase,
We met each other in a maze.
He's got a really big brain,
You see, he wants to drive a crane.

He loves jam tarts,
He likes doing lots of farts.
He likes picking his nose
And has very big toes.

Tom Spoors (11)
Huish Episcopi Primary School

A GIRL

There's this girl that dresses so fine,
Always drinking red and white wine.
She goes outside when it is light,
Always playing with a multicoloured kite.
Her mum says, 'In,'
When it's getting dim.
She reads a book in her head
And then she goes to bed.

There's this boy that messes about,
He's got a big loud mouth and he always shouts,
He plays on his skateboard all day long
And says he's done nothing wrong.
He slips himself into his PJs
And sleeps until the next day.
And now you know
How it really goes!

Kelly Frome (10)
Huish Episcopi Primary School

A DREAM

A dream; an imaginary cloud to me,
It brings happy memories of past times,
And how life could be.

A dream; takes you on a trip,
Over hills and mountains,
On a train, a bus or a ship.

A dream; is in your mind,
A made-up storyline,
Sometimes they are evil, but normally kind.

A dream; is forgotten when you wake up,
It can never be caught,
Not even in a bag, a tissue or a cup.

A dream sometimes turns to reality.

Sophie Miller (10)
Huish Episcopi Primary School

THE SKEWBALD HORSE

The skewbald horse
Is called Tallulah and she likes her food.
Energetic, cheeky, fluffy,
Soft as the tropical sands,
As big as an elephant,
She makes me feel wanted,
Like an important part of life.
The skewbald horse,
It makes me feel free.

Harriet Forster (10)
Huish Episcopi Primary School

It's An . . .

Intent starer,
Fish scarer,
Shooting flash,
Sapphire dash,
Immobile fisher,
Never a misser.
Plump ball,
Whistling call,
Spectacular diver,
Predator skiver,
River's jewel,
Above the pool,
Patient sitter,
It's a . . . kingfisher.

Amy Sweetman (10)
Keinton Mandeville Primary School

It's A . . .

Music rocker,
Hip hop knocker,
R and B banger,
Rock slammer,
Rapping beat,
Feel the heat,
Dancing feel,
Electric eel,
Thumping bass,
Quick pace,
Note whisk,
It's a . . . mini disc.

Alex Poyner (11)
Keinton Mandeville Primary School

IT'S A . . .

Net spinner,
Bird's dinner,
Swift glider,
Good hider,
Very hairy,
Also scary,
Monster tall,
Maybe small,
Tiny gap,
Sticky trap,
Air rider,
Web resider,
Corner sider,
It's a . . . spider.

Tonya Greenidge (11)
Keinton Mandeville Primary School

IT'S A

Long leaper,
Water creeper,
Super swimmer
He's a winner!
He's so slimy,
Rather grimy,
Loud croak,
Scares some folk,
Pond hog,
It's a . . . *frog.*

Thomas Cella (11)
Keinton Mandeville Primary School

IT'S A ...

Fish lover,
Caring mother,
Lazy sleeper,
Silent creeper,
Bad loser,
String user,
Peaceful singer,
Bird bringer,
Loves dinners,
Hates swimmers,
Soft cuddles,
Never in muddles,
Normally fat,
It's a . . . cat.

Inina Opstrup (10)
Keinton Mandeville Primary School

MY NUMBER POEM

I was pleased to have my *11th* birthday on Monday,
I've just finished being *10* now.
I know I have to be in school before *9* o'clock in the morning,
And I'm not often *18*,
But we were diverted through *7* road.
All the twists and turns made me car*6*,
But listening to *5* on the radio soon cheered me up,
4 I'm their biggest fan!
I tried to think of *3* different things to dress-up as for our 'Maths Day',
But it was *2* late, so here I am,
The only *1* who made up a silly poem!

Tiffany Trewin (11)
Kewstoke Primary School

SWINGING SHELL

A tiger-pod,
A stripy cluster,
A big muncher,
A leaf destroyer,
A shrivelled bag,
A hard nut,
A flitter beauty,
A faint flutter,
A flutter flier,
A proud beauty,
A catalogue to make me
A butterfly.

Jed Collis (10)
Long Sutton Primary School

RAINBOW WINGS

A tiger pad,
A stripy cluster,
A large muncher,
A leaf destroyer,
A shrivelled bag,
A hanging moon,
A faint flutter,
A burst of beauty,
A cloud explorer,
A flowing wonder,
A catalogue to make me
A butterfly.

Catalina Moffat (11)
Long Sutton Primary School

HIGH FLYER!

A tiger-pod,
A stripy cluster,
A big muncher,
A leaf destroyer,
A high camper,
A little glistener,
A bursting beauty,
A flying flower,
A cloud explorer,
A perfect take-off.
I am a butterfly.

James Kew (10
Long Sutton Primary School

AUTUMN

Leaves fall,
Crunch, crunch, crumble.
Children playing in leaves,
Hedgehogs hibernate, snuffle, snuffle, snore,
Autumn.

Jane Rieveley (10)
Long Sutton Primary School

WINTER'S GOING

Snowmen melting
In the exhausting sun,
Turning into icy water,
Winter.

Matthew Cardwell (10)
Long Sutton Primary School

AUTUMN

Autumn,
Listen,
Firework launch,
Listen to the leaves fall,
Can you hear the people holler,
Boom, bang!

Nathan Norris (10)
Long Sutton Primary School

AUTUMN DAWN

Dawn breaks,
Crunch, crunch, crunch, steps
Sound in the early morn.
Leaves drop, hovering slowly down,
Day comes.

Stephen Wall (10)
Long Sutton Primary School

WINTER IS GOING

Winter,
Snowmen melting
In the exhausting sun,
Turning into icy water,
Winter.

Adrian Dyer (11)
Long Sutton Primary School

CHRISTMAS DAY

Unwrap
Lots of presents,
Yum, delicious turkey,
Lots of excitement all day round,
Goodnight.

Georgina Phillips (11)
Long Sutton Primary School

AUTUMN DAYS

Leaves fall,
Birds are singing,
Fireworks in the sky.
Guy Fawkes is burning in the night,
Autumn.

Tom Jones (11)
Long Sutton Primary School

AUTUMN

Listen,
Fireworks launching,
Listen to the leaves falling,
Can you hear the people holler,
Boom, *bang!*

Oliver Dent (9)
Long Sutton Primary School

AUTUMN

Autumn
Leaves fall,
Crunch, crunch, crumble.
Children playing in leaves,
Hedgehogs hibernate, snuffle, snore,
Autumn.

Abigail Smith (11)
Long Sutton Primary School

CHRISTMAS EVE

Sleeping
And waiting for
The dawn, wishing presents
Will come from Santa and Rudolf,
Whoopee!

Charlotte Hole (10)
Long Sutton Primary School

SNOW DAYS

Winter,
Snow time at last,
Crunching through the white snow,
Snow fights, snowmen, fun all day long,
Snow time.

Isabel Ronchi (10)
Long Sutton Primary School

AUTUMN

Leaves falling,
Children playing,
Bonfire burning, smoking,
Everybody loves autumn,
Cool time.

Amy Wicks (9)
Long Sutton Primary School

SNOWY DAYS

Falling,
Soft, cold snowflakes,
White, fat snowmen standing,
Melting into the ground they go,
Sinking.

Lydia Cox (11)
Long Sutton Primary School

WINTER'S NIGHT

Midnight,
Cold and spooky,
Carpeted in white fur,
Silence settling all around,
Morning.

Amy Collins (10)
Long Sutton Primary School

THE END OF WINTER

The snow,
Melting away,
Spring is coming, hip hooray,
The winter's creeping back again,
Some day.

John Barlow (10)
Long Sutton Primary School

WINTER EVENING

Crisp snow
Breaks underfoot,
Tall trees swing back and forth,
All the castle ghosts are active,
Creepy.

Matthew Keech (10)
Long Sutton Primary School

AUTUMN

A   utumn is fun,
U   mbrellas are pulled through the air,
T   rees are losing their leaves,
U   p in the trees, conker cases pop open,
M   igrating birds fly south,
N   ature is everywhere.

Luke Ward (7)
Millfield Prep School

HORSES ARE FAST

H orses are fast and elegant,
O ver the hills, horses gallop:
R olling and playing, jumping high,
S oaring across the plains and prairies, I can't see them.
E very horse shall be great and elegant;
S ave the horses from hunters and don't kill them!

A ging for years, they live twenty years;
R acing along the fields, they are, horses;
E ating in the evening shall make horses strong for
   another day's work.

F lying over the ground, as if they've wings,
A s if there is a blur, it is horses galloping;
S o very fast a horse can gallop,
T oo fast for a car's speedometer.

Grace Hills (8)
Millfield Prep School

ANIMALS

Horses go clip-clop on the pavement of the street
While snails go slithering over a brick, that takes them a minute,
Cows go 'moo' when you go past,
Pigs lay down and go 'oink-oink'.
Lions roar and stand up with bushy hair all around their faces,
While cats go 'miaow' and start to purr.
Dogs go 'woof' and pull at ladies' skirts,
While humans just go round saying, 'What shall we get today?'

Beatrice Wood (7)
Millfield Prep School

PUPPIES

You can get puppies all around the world.
You can get small puppies and big puppies,
They are all different colours.
I love puppies,
They are small and clumsy and they roll about everywhere,
All of them are different breeds.
I like bull-terriers, chocolate Labradors, spaniels, Jack Russells
and Dalmatians.

Lily Parkinson (7)
Millfield Prep School

NOWHERE, SCILLY
(Nowhere is a hamlet on St Marys in the Isles of Scilly)

I hate it when grown-ups say,
'Where do you go to school?
So I say, 'Nowhere.'
'Nowhere? Nowhere? Of course you go to school!' they say.
'I go to school in Nowhere,' I say.
'Where is Nowhere then, child?' they ask,
and I reply, 'Nowhere, Scilly!'

Alexandra Franklin (9)
Millfield Prep School

TWIGLET

A golden hare streaking through the grass,
An elegant deer flying over ditches,
A small red fox trotting boldly along,
A faithful friend, always there for me.

She lies by the fire, toasting her tummy,
She hunts rabbits in the meadows and hedgerows,
She races along the footpaths, feet flying fast,
She greets me at the door with a leap and a lick.

Felicity Whitehouse (10)
Millfield Prep School

DOLPHINS

D iving, splashing,
O ceans, crashing,
L apping water silently,
P rancing very prettily,
H oping for a sunny day,
I n dreams she'll sit there and say,
'N othing ever bothers me
S wimming elegantly.'

Holly Aungiers (10)
Millfield Prep School

BROTHERS' RULES

1 Always let them answer the phone,
2 Don't fight with them,
3 Always let them kiss Mum first,
4 Don't touch their stuff,
5 Always fill their drink up,
6 Always clean their room,
7 Let them in the front,
8 Always let them do the fun things first.

Tiphanie Bintcliffe (8)
Millfield Prep School

COOL KIDS

The kids at our school are a really cool bunch,
But if you're not their friend, they'll eat you for lunch.

There's Clare, my best mate, and she's really cool,
She's so marvellous that she rocks the school!

There's Edmund, my boyfriend and he's trendy,
He's really cute and he is always with me.

There's William, who's nice,
And he keeps pet mice.

There's Lucy, the racing car, as fast as lightning,
She's speedy, like an eagle with two white wings.

There's Tiphanie, the dancer, who twirls and rocks,
At discos she's a funky fox.

There's Princess Coombes, a groovy chick,
She can order us about, with an easy flick!

And best of all, last of all, there is me,
Great, wicked, wild and groovy.

Me and my mates are totally *funky!*

Christie Jones (8)
Millfield Prep School

POOLS

P   ools are fun to splash in,
O   and if you want to relax, just go where the thrusters are,
O   and it's lovely where the current is.
L   ie in the pool too long and you'll get wrinkles.
S   ome pools come in different shapes and sizes.

Hugh Wyatt (8)
Millfield Prep School

MY FRIENDLY SPIRIT

My friendly spirit always follows me.
He eats what I want to eat,
He drinks what I want to drink,
He plays what I want to play.
He does everything I want to do,
He keeps me company wherever I go.

He climbs trees,
He runs,
He eats,
He sleeps,
He talks.

I am the only person who knows
My friendly spirit
And he is my best friend.

Henry Fabre (8)
Millfield Prep School

SKELETON

S   omething in the dark,
K   ind of scary!
E   ating your
L   egs!
E   veryone is scared . . .
T   he skeleton is sniffing you
O   n your bed.
N   o one whisper! Sh, sh, sh.

Zoe Wall (9)
Millfield Prep School

ALERTISQUIRT

Alertisquirt, old and grey
Trampling everything in his way.
He's very alert
And loves to squirt.
It's fun for him,
With a tail so thin,
A trunk very strong
And legs so long,
As he speeds from the fire,
The flames leap higher.
He runs for a bath
As wicked hyenas laugh.
A mouse is so small,
Compared to him, so tall.
For many years
He's flapped his ears.
At eleven feet high,
He reaches way into the sky.

Max Adams (8)
Millfield Prep School

AN ACCIDENT

Mum was walking through the door,
Spilt some milk on the floor.
She wiped it up, but no, it made a stain,
So off she went to buy some cleaner.
She went back home,
She tried again and it worked.

Daniel Lewis-Williams (8)
Millfield Prep School

FOOTBALL

When the match was beginning,
The crowd started singing.
When the first goal was scored,
The crowd, how they roared.
A player went down,
A man got a card,
The air became heavy,
Whistles were blown.
They sought to bring order
To this crowd of disorder.
Too late, charging, bombarding,
The crowd stormed the pitch.
The game, how it ended,
Despite the offended,
The players forgave the ref
And trooped to the kitchen
To greet the chef.

Harry West-Taylor (10)
Millfield Prep School

JAGUAR

Jaguar racing through the sky,
A flying aeroplane
Orbiting the sun.
Under clouds, over seas,
Around buildings, around trees,
Ripping down branches
With its speed,
That's the Jaguar's ability.

Piers Denning (9)
Millfield Prep School

SNOWY DAY

It's snowing today,
I'm going outside,
I want to knock the snowman down.

I put on my hat,
I put on my gloves,
I put on everything I need.

The wind blows in my face,
It makes me cold,
The snow is just too deep and slushy.

My umbrella's blown off,
I've got snow in my boots,
And my feet are absolutely freezing!

I think I might go inside!

Lucy Etherington (8)
Millfield Prep School

MUSHROOMS

M ushrooms, yuck, they're sick!
U nder my lettuce on my plate you'll find some hiding there,
S hrivelled up, yellow and wet,
H orrible and mushy, they'll make you shiver.
R otten, disgusting mushrooms, no one can like them.
O kay, some people like them, but I don't,
O ld mushrooms, mouldy and revolting.
M ummy makes me eat them,
S o I'm going on a diet.

Megan Hill (9)
Millfield Prep School

LUNCH BOX

Lunch, munch, crash, crunch!
Jenny's got ice cream and chocolate beans,
Will has an apple and custard creams.
Peter scoffs crisps and pizza too,
Lucy shouts, 'I won't sit with you!'
Chris drinks juice and Pepsi pop,
Jo tried but he just couldn't stop.
Chloe had burger and French-fried chips,
Claire had olives without the pips.
George forgot his lunch again,
Mrs Pots got angry and so did Ken!
But my own lunch is best of all,
Banana crunch and chocolate, cool!
Kids in school will shout and yell,
'Give us some or we'll go and tell!'

Sarah Woods (9)
Millfield Prep School

MY OLD HOUSE

The carpet rucks,
The chairs squeak,
The oven burns,
The cupboards crack,
The windows shatter,
The front door slams,
The lights flicker,
The stairs creak,
My shoulders quiver
When I step into my old house.

Jack McNeil (9)
Millfield Prep School

RUGBY

Crash! Bang! Ouch! Oooh!
Are the words that describe a rugby do.
Rugby is a rough old game,
Which can sometimes be a huge shame.
Broken arm, broken neck,
Injuries I can surely check.
Three in the scrum, also eight,
I've got a rugby match today,
I mustn't be late.
They could be big, they could be small,
They could be tiny, they could be tall.
Rugby I could never hate,
A bit like strawberries, which I just ate.

Toby Lett (9)
Millfield Prep School

HAPPINESS

Happiness is when the sun is beaming through your window.
It's when you take a big bite out of your juicy, red apple.
Happiness is when you win a sparkling medal
And when you have a party and get lots of wonderful pressies.
Happiness is being captain for all of the sports,
Feeling like you're going to explode with joy.
Eating chicken nuggets and chips all week!
Knowing that your dog is having puppies the next day.
Happiness is winning a match
And being given lots of sweets.
Happiness is when it's the end of school
And being head boy.

William Heywood (9)
Millfield Prep School

SNOW

I wake up in my bed,
Morning has come to play.
I look outside my window
And I see along the grass a long
White, glistening blanket of snow.
'Whoo!' I shout, 'Snow has come at last.'
I run to my wardrobe, grab my snow suit
And my gloves, my hat, my scarf and my boots.
I race downstairs and pull everything on.
I open the door and as I'm going out
I yell to my mum,
'I'm going to see the snow!'
I run outside and look around into the white world,
Then suddenly I turn around and see my sister
With a snowball in her hand.
She throws one at me;
I throw one at her.
We start a snowball fight, but too late,
Night has come already.
We have been having so much fun.
We run inside, shove off our boots
And run into the kitchen where our mum is.
'Come on you two, it's time to eat,
And after that, it's bedtime
So you can get your sleep!'

Elisabeth Foulkes (9)
Millfield Prep School

RUGBY

It's the start of the match and the whistle goes,
The players are all friends or foes,
It's a great pass out and the wing scores,
Suddenly all the crowd roars.
Soon enough it's the half-time break,
Who knows what decisions they will make.
Will they attack, or will they defend?
All will come clear towards the end.
A bad foul gets a red card,
Surely this player should be barred.
Finally the whistle goes, all the losers start to moan,
All the crowd want to go home.
It was a great game of rugby that day,
I just wish my team could play.

Tom Moore (10)
Millfield Prep School

DAD

Dad is very ill in hospital,
He is in intensive care.
He's had a terrible heart operation.
Mummy's in London comforting him.
I feel so worried about him.
Dad, I hope you get better soon.

David Littman (9)
Millfield Prep School

AZTECS

T enochtitlan is an Aztec city,
E mperor of the Aztecs is Montezuma,
N o people have houses like Montezuma did.
O n Lake Texcoco they built Tenochtitlan,
C auseway is the way to get into Tenochtitlan,
H ulzdopochtlin, is an Aztec god,
T emples are where they sacrifice people.
I ndians paid tributes to the Aztecs,
T ribes fight the Aztecs.
L ake Texcoco was under Tenochtitlan.
A ztecs were a Mexican tribe,
N obles were rich people.

Alastair Wall (8)
Millfield Prep School

AT HALLOWE'EN

At Hallowe'en I saw the queen,
Dressed as a witch, she made me twitch
And shout, 'Witch!'
And I ran as fast as I could.
'Help! Help!' I cried,
My eye was twitching, my head was twitching,
The witch was after me.
'Come here my dear,' she said,
'No fear!' I cried,
I turned around and heard her sound,
'Boo!' It was my mother.

Chloë Warren (9)
Millfield Prep School

CATS

Cats can be big or small,
Massive, tiny and lots more.
Some have big teeth,
Some have small feet.
Some smile, some are wild,
Some chase, some race.
Some are mean, some are clean.
Some have babies, some have rabies.

Charlie Martin (8)
Millfield Prep School

DOGS

Dogs are fun to play with,
Dogs are very good,
But dogs are best when they are hairy.
Dogs shake themselves when they are wet.
Dogs are the best animals in the world.
My favourite dog is a Jack Russell.

Edmund Rhind-Tutt (8)
Millfield Prep School

MY BIG, FAT ELEPHANT

My big, fat elephant stomps around,
He makes supper at teatime.
He falls through the floor at bedtime
And when he cries, he floods the whole house
With one big, fat tear.

Clare Haskins (8)
Millfield Prep School

GOOD FEELINGS

Good feelings are when you get a new friend,
You feel happy when you have just won an egg-and-spoon race.
I feel happy when I'm on a trampoline,
Feeling like I can touch the sky.
My cousin felt happy when she got a new little sister.
Everybody feels happy when you're smiling.

Emma Johnson (8)
Millfield Prep School

THE WEATHER

Wind is so noisy, it howls like a wolf,
Sun is so hot, time to play golf.
Rain is so wet, it soaks you and me,
Snow is such fun, I'll go out with glee.
It's time to say bye as it's getting cloudy,
So bye for now until I say *howdy!*

Richard Gabb (9)
Millfield Prep School

BIG SISTERS

Big sisters are sometimes fun,
Big sisters are sometimes sick
Because they have boyfriends
That they always kiss.
I say, 'Yuck!'
But she says, 'Shut up!'

Shakira Cropper (8)
Millfield Prep School

POPPING BEANS

Popping beans are my favourite.
Looking at them makes me jump.
I watch them whiz along the floor,
Bump, bump, bump, bump, bump!

They never stop their popping,
Bouncing up into the sky,
Reaching up higher and higher,
Like a happy butterfly.

The popping beans are noisy,
They pop lots and lots and lots.
I'll tell you what they sound like,
A big bowl of Coco Pops.

Laura Coates (9)
Millfield Prep School

MY GREAT, OLD HOME

In the drawers is secret money,
In the icy fridge is runny honey,
All seven kittens, snoozing about,
In the pond, a big, large trout.
On the swing, my little brother,
In the sun is my drunk mother,
In rattling cages are all dad's pigeons,
My brother calls them pidgwidens.
Up the stairs I quietly tread,
Up to the high old bed.

Victoria Berryman (7)
Millfield Prep School

SNOW CLOUDS

S   parkling crystal manna, falling from the sky,
N   othing can resist it, falling from the sky,
O   ver mountains it blows, falling from the sky,
W   hite crystal manna, falling from the sky.

C   overing everything in a white blanket,
L   ying on the ground,
O   ver hills,
U   nder bridges,
D   ie it will not,
S   ettling on the earth.

Christopher Deakin (9)
Millfield Prep School

THE SUNKEN WRECK

There the ship lies in its sleep,
Far beneath the upper deep.
Some people say it holds some treasure,
Some people say it's just the weather.
The glinting sun upon the deck,
It's a dark and spooky endless wreck.
Some people say it's made of gold,
But I just think it's a lot of mould.
There it shall lay and there it shall keep,
The sunken treasures of the deep!

Charlotte Barraclough (10)
Millfield Prep School

DOG'S SLEEP

My old dog did not want to play with anyone,
Not even with another dog, like his brother.
His brother was jumping all over him,
His younger brother Milo, was so tired, he gave up
And slept on top of him.
My favourite dogs are Labradors and Jack Russells.

Keith Showering (8)
Millfield Prep School

RAT

The raving reveller scampers swiftly;
A lazy chatterbox,
Pipe-sprinter, patter, patter,
A peanut farmer -
The shoulder-sitting alarm clock.
A friendly vandal,
Cheeky soaker
Clatter and splash!
The good-deed doer
Is a sound sleeper.
He's an acrobat! Scuttle and bound!
Champion chewer
This Olympic snoozer
Is an agile washer -
The ridiculous mate!

Megan Manley (10)
Redstart Primary School

THE MONTHS OF THE YEAR

January welcomes the new coming year
and dads try not to drink so much beer

February includes Valentine's Day
so watch out, boys, we're heading your way

March is the third month of the year
I can smell the chocolate coming quite near

April showers keep falling on my head
I think I'll be better in my nice warm bed

May is here, April has been
Dancers are ready on the village green

June is warm, summer is coming
The busy bees are already humming

July is boiling, paddling pools are out
The freezing water is making children shout

August is my tenth birthday
Schoolchildren are at home, hip, hip hooray

September I am finally a Year Six
I can stop all the playground pushes and kicks

October already, it's Hallowe'en night
Pumpkins are lit, I'll give you a fright

November the fifth, the fireworks whoosh by
The smoke from the bonfire flies through the sky

December finally, it's Christmas Day
I sit down and have a really, long play.

Jessica Simpson (9)
Redstart Primary School

THE MAN IN THE CORRIDOR

Sneaking from shadow to shadow.
A hand like a goblin.
A cape like a puma's skin.
A shadow nightmare.
Something at his feet.
A huge, fighting soldier.
The muscles of bricks.
Never-ceasing darkness.
Always draining happiness.
No one goes there.
Not the bravest man.
Nor the strongest champion.
So the unsolved mystery.
The *man in the corridor* remains.

Joshua Kilbride (10)
Redstart Primary School

LOOKING OUT THE WINDOW

Look out the window,
See what you can see.
See the rain, hear the wind,
Watch the trees bend.

'Bbrrr, I feel cold.'

When you look out the window
To see what you can see,
Watch the people run to and fro.
'Bbrrr! I bet it's cold.'

Stephanie Wells-Burr (9)
Redstart Primary School

STORM

Inky black clouds put out the sun
With the wind destroying the flame
The hand in the sky gathers the water
And then tips out the rain

The bowl in the sea with a mast and a sail
Is tossed about like a ball
The jagged rock all covered in spray
Turns into a danger for all

The boat hits the rock with a rip and a tear
And the water comes in like a storm
That unlucky ship with the old wooden planks
Soon to be tattered and torn

From inside the waves there comes a faint splash
That is very nearly not heard
Suddenly a shout rings through the storm
'Help, help! Man overboard!'

Kathryn Hunt (9)
Redstart Primary School

DOG

There you lie in your bed
Things running through your head.
Dog running around the garden,
Playing on the kitchen floor all day.
Her tail is as black as night.
Her eyes are burning bright.

Kerrie Winter (11)
Redstart Primary School

SNAIL

He is as slow as a worm.
He is as strong as a stag
And he has an armoured shell.
A pest in the garden.
A nightmare for gardeners.
All different shapes and sizes.
A shy little creature.
Enemy of birds!
He leaves a trail to remember him.

Alastair Haste (10)
Redstart Primary School

FRIENDS

Friends are for sharing with.
Friends are for playing with
If you didn't have friends you would be bored.
If you didn't have friends you would be lonely.
But I've got friends better than that.
I've got a friend that I will have forever.

Kayleigh Vaux (8)
Redstart Primary School

THE FOX

The predator at night
As fast as light.
His red coat is like fire
Body shaped like a pillow
But claws like a sharp knife.

Nathan Skyrme (10)
Redstart Primary School

WIGGLY WORM

I am a wiggly worm
I am a wiggly worm

I sometimes make you squirm

I am a wiggly worm
I am a wiggly worm

I wriggle along singing a song
Some people think I pong

I am a wiggly worm
I am a wiggly worm

I live underground where I can't be found
It's so very dark and I can't hear a sound

I am a wiggly worm
I am a wiggly worm

Jade Dunning (8)
Redstart Primary School

LION

Its teeth are as sharp as a pickaxe
His fur is like a bush
With a flame on his tail
Its eyes are spies,
In the grass is his prey
Then the prey runs and the lion is going to get it.
Now his prey is dead and he tears some flesh
And has his dinner.

Karl Fletcher (10)
Redstart Primary School

STORMS

Stormy weather,
Ships crashing,
Men dying,
Women crying,
Thunder banging,
Lightning frightening,
Bang, boom, bang . . .

Stormy weather,
Hurricanes coming,
Men dying,
Children crying,
Thunder banging,
Lightning frightening,
Bang, boom, bang!

Rachel Cox (8)
Redstart Primary School

I WISH I WAS A DRAGON

I wish I was a dragon with fire like the burning sun
I wish I was a dragon with scales like the grass in the breeze
                              and a tail like an arrow.
I wish I was a dragon with big, brown eyes like the middle
                              of a sunflower.
I wish I was a dragon with feet like thunder.
I wish I was a dragon with a nose like two wormholes.
I wish I was a dragon with ears like a shark's fin.
I wish I was a

                dragon!

Marsha Hall (7)
Redstart Primary School

I HAD A SCARE!

I was asleep
Then I woke up with a scare
Somebody was flying in the air
It was white, it was big
And it was *scary!*
I woke up my mum
But she said there was nothing there,
She went back to sleep
But I still had a scare
I shut my door
And went back to sleep
I heard my mum snoring
That gave me the creeps.

Megan Butt (8)
Redstart Primary School

EXCITEMENT WITH THE WAVES

See the waves rolling to the shore getting ready to break,
making the ocean more rough.
See the foam whirling onto the sand and rocks colliding
against people's faces, by the aggressive winds.
See the children running where a wave would break,
before the delighted sound of the waves makes them excited.
See the people swimming over the towering waves, waiting
for the continuous waves over and over again.
See a mysterious creature appear like it's bobbing over the waves
it is a camouflaged armoury of weapons.

Sophie Harris (10)
Redstart Primary School

WHAT IS IT?

As fast as a lion,
As small as a mouse,
Cats' prey, look out!
Have you guessed yet?
Of course, it's a

　　　　　rat!

Esther Brown (8)
Redstart Primary School

CAT

His teeth are as yellow as glowing rays.
His stripes are like black tunnels.
His fur is spiky.
His eyes are fireballs in the night.
His tail puckers with fright.
He is the colour of darkness, *beware!*

Abbie Bide (10)
Redstart Primary School

THE DOG

It barks like thunder rumbling in the sky.
Someone knocks on the door.
You see the creature run to the door like lightning.
You see his bones stretching to get to the door.
It is a white creature streaking from the sky.

Sarah Bishop (10)
Redstart Primary School

TORTOISE

The ancient acceptable alien
Is a nearly nimble-nipper.
The crawling, crunching tortoise
Is a rough, wrinkly rock.
A tower-towing racer
And a moody aged time-waster.

Joanna Dymel (11)
Redstart Primary School

LATE KATE

There was a little girl called Kate
Who was always late
Her teacher said
She must be in bed
That little girl called Kate.

Emilee Glenn (8)
Redstart Primary School

I WISH

I wish I had a wishing tree
and the wishes fall on me.
I wish I had a wishing tree
and the wishes would grow upon the leaves.

Robert Gibbs (8)
Redstart Primary School

THE SUN

The sun's
shining brightly
the clouds
have gone away.
The rain
won't come back
until the
4th of May.

The blue
sky is staring
I wonder
what it means?
Will it rain
will it cloud
or will it
be sunny?

Whatever
the weather is
it might
be sunny,
rainy, or
even a rainbow
it does
not matter
I will always
love the sky
how it is.

Samantha Curnock (8)
Redstart Primary School

ROBIN HOOD

Robin Hood was very good
He lived in a forest in Sherwood
He stole from rich and gave to poor
And then went back to do some more
His merry men helped as well
Even though some did smell
All were wearing tunics and tights
They were a match for the king's own knights
That was the story of Robin Hood
I hope it was very good!

Megan Emery (9)
Redstart Primary School

UPON MY STAR

Little star shining so bright,
Twinkling in the dark, black night.
Can you see me from so far?
Are you listening, little star?

Will you grant my wish tonight
And send it to me on a beam of light?

While you shine with the moon so high,
I will watch you every night
And when I have to go to bed,
You are watching like a friend.

You get up every night for me,
Are you shining just for me?
When I look at you I find
The magic in your secret key.

Louisa Mair (9)
St Aldhelm's CE Primary School, Doulting

MY STAR

I look upon my star tonight,
It shines so bright
Upon the Earth.
This star is worth
A lot to me.

Little star in the sky I see,
Are you shining just for me?
You're the first star to shine at night
And you shine so bright,
Giving your light
To all the children of the world tonight.

Charlotte Mair (9)
St Aldhelm's CE Primary School, Doulting

MY BUG

Mr Bug upon my wall
doesn't bother me at all.
But if he crawls in my bed,
then that is something to be said.

I would not like him to bite my toes
and I would not like him to tickle my nose.
So please, Mr Bug, stay on the wall,
then you won't scare me,
no, not at all.

Cianni Brook (9)
St Aldhelm's CE Primary School, Doulting

MY HAMSTER

My hamster's grey and fluffy,
Her name is Misty Moo,
She has two best friends,
My cats, Lucy and Boo-Boo.

They sit at night and lick their lips,
They dream of hamster and chocolate dip.
Misty gnaws her cage at night,
I think my cats give her a fright.

She runs quite fast and jumps up high,
Sometimes I think she'd like to fly.
She looks at me when I say goodnight,
Then turns around and snuggles down tight.

I love my hamster very much,
I think she's really sweet.
She always looks so beautiful
And loves her peanut treats.

Lauren Luxford (9)
St Aldhelm's CE Primary School, Doulting

BEING ILL

One day my brother called Bill
Rolled up a very big hill.
I know it sounds nonsense,
But it made him unconscious.
For months he was seriously ill.

Michael Barnett (11)
St Aldhelm's CE Primary School, Doulting

MY RABBIT

She's my funny rabbit,
She loves me very much,
She lives in the sun outside,
In her bunny hutch.

I take her in the house,
She loves running around,
She doesn't like high places,
She likes it on the ground.

When my friend is at my house,
We always play with her,
In the afternoon we sit
And stroke her golden fur.

She really makes me happy,
Mum says she's just some hair,
Nobody can say that,
Because she's mine, so there!

Sarah Ford (8)
St Aldhelm's CE Primary School, Doulting

IN OLD TIMES

In old times of pots and pans,
When people had unsteady hands,
Blog the caveman said, 'Ug, ug,'
Which clearly meant he had dug
Up carrots and turnips and things of that kind,
And anything else that he could find.

One day he found a long pink thing,
He thought nobody would have one, not even the King.
So he brought it home to his trusty wife,
Who had the biggest, sharpest knife.
He said, 'Sauce of ages, want sauce of ages,'
And then with much greatness, he named them sausages!

Sam Moulton (10)
St Aldhelm's CE Primary School, Doulting

ANY DOG

Big dogs, small dogs,
I don't really care.
Tall dogs, short dogs,
Ones with fluffy hair.

White dogs, black dogs,
One with a crinkled tail.
Fat dogs, thin dogs,
Those that really smell.

Poodles, Afghans,
Alsatians and bulldogs,
Yorkshire terriers
And some that look like frogs.

But when it comes to choosing,
I find myself in a fog,
Cos if I really think of it,
I don't mind any dog.

Bethany Manders (10)
St Aldhelm's CE Primary School, Doulting

WORD PICTURE

Short words,
Long words,
Some-can-sing-a-song words.

Sweet words,
Rude words
Some-get-in-a-mood words.

Weak words,
Strong words,
Some-like-to-show-off words.

Silly words,
Clever words,
Now make some of *your own* words.

Suzy Corner (9)
St Aldhelm's CE Primary School, Doulting

POEM OF COLOURS

Red is the colour of Santa's clothes,
Blue is the colour of the sky,
Green is the colour of the grass,
Yellow is the colour of corn.
White is the colour of the clouds,
Silver is the colour of a 10p coin,
Gold is the colour of a shining crown,
Brown is the colour of a tree's branch.
Purple is the colour of a juicy plum,
Orange is the colour of the sun.

Katie Burr (8)
St Aldhelm's CE Primary School, Doulting

MY LITTLE BROTHER

When I was a little boy, my mummy grew a tummy,
Then suddenly I turned around
And there was something sucking on a dummy.

It screamed and screamed and then it had a paddy,
All you could get out of it was,
'Oh, I want my daddy.'

All it did was eat and drink and then fill its nappy,
But mummy said that's alright,
As long as he is a happy chappy.

Nathan Young (10)
St Aldhelm's CE Primary School, Doulting

MY LITTLE PONY

I had a little pony,
Whose life was awfully lonely.

So off I went one summer's day
And bought myself a dapple-grey.

My little pony was so pleased,
He jumped about and coughed and sneezed.

Around the field they both did play
And so were happy all the day.

Kathryn Cawsey (9)
St Aldhelm's CE Primary School, Doulting

NIGHT LOVE

The moon shone,
Then the mysterious rider
Came, and then was gone.

Every night he came
As I watched out of my window.
Every night he shattered my window frame.

One night I found he was silver-white,
Then he looked to my window
And rode off to the night.

A year later he came back,
He said, 'Come, my love.'
We rode off to the black.

Louisa Garbett (9)
St Aldhelm's CE Primary School, Doulting

MYSTICAL AND MAGICAL

Mystical and magical
Treasure lies beneath the sand,
Hidden by the ruby dragon's land.

Their beds are made of jewellery
And diamonds and emeralds.
Small beds for the young,
Big beds for the elderly.

Their waistcoats are made of gold and silver,
To show off their fancy ways.
Beneath the blanket made of jewels
For hundreds of years they lay.

Esme Stevens (10)
St Aldhelm's CE Primary School, Doulting

THE ALIEN UNDERPANTS

They're square and spotty,
Multicoloured and dotty,
Hypnotising,
Poltergeisting,
Alien underpants.

Floated down from space,
Should have seen my face,
Knocked me out,
But I soon came about.
Alien underpants.

Blown off the line,
Chosen at random,
Or design,
They abducted me,
The alien underpants.

James Ford (10)
St Aldhelm's CE Primary School, Doulting

WEATHER WITH FEELING

The sky is in my head,
The stars are in my heart,
The rain is in my tears
And my life is soon to start.

The clouds are my icy cheeks,
The sun is in my soul,
The lightning is my rage
And when they come together,
They make a whole.

Millie Ayton-Moon (10)
St Aldhelm's CE Primary School, Doulting

SPACE

I'm going to zoom
In the stars.
I'll visit the moon,
Maybe Mars.

The sun is so hot
And very light,
I like it a lot,
But it is very bright.

Look at the moon.
Is it really cheese?
I think I'll fly up there
And give it a squeeze.

Fiona Stevens (8)
St Aldhelm's CE Primary School, Doulting

MY DOG

Golden and big,
Furry and strong,
It runs around the house
All day long,
Wagging its tail
And hurries along.
It jumps up high
And rolls from side to side.
I love to cuddle him,
He's my best friend,
He's my dog.

Jack Vaughan (8)
St Aldhelm's CE Primary School, Doulting

HOW I FEEL

How I feel about the tears of my friend,
The unhappiness in her heart,
The children in the playground
And the tears which have begun.

The thunder and the lightning,
And most of the time I'm frightened,
The pounding of my heart,
I hope that I'll get home.

My class are really cool friends,
I hope that they'll take care of me,
My life is to be given a chance
And that is all I hope to see.

The sun covers up the rainy days
And all the times I have been sad,
I need all the friends I can have,
The times I've been sad.

The twister in my mind!

Jessica Wilkins (11)
St Aldhelm's CE Primary School, Doulting

CAT FLEAS

In the cat's hairs are fleas,
They like to eat your cat's hairs
And eat your peas,
And drink your tea,
So watch out for the fleas,
They like to eat peas.

Joseph Niblett (9)
St Joseph's RC Primary School, Burnham-on-Sea

STARS

The stars flicker
In the moonlit sky,
Stars drifting,
Flashing as they fly.

Stars twinkle,
Coming out at night.
When the sun comes up,
They disappear out of sight.

Stars dazzle
When the moon comes up.
They make different shapes,
Socks, shoes, a cup.

Stars fade
As night goes away.
Sun comes up,
It is day.

Hayley Mear (10)
St Joseph's RC Primary School, Burnham-on-Sea

I LOVE DRAGONS

Dragons are green,
Dragons are blue,
Dragons breathe fire
And hide down the loo.
Dragons are scary
And friendly too,
I love dragons
And so should you.

Millie Taylor (9)
St Joseph's RC Primary School, Burnham-on-Sea

ONE DARK, DARK NIGHT

I walked in the woods
One *dark, dark* night,
I heard a rustling ahead of me.
It got closer and closer,
An owl it must be.

I walked in the woods
One *dark, dark* night,
I saw a shadow ahead of me.
It got closer and closer,
A fox it must be.

I walked in the woods
One *dark, dark* night,
I heard a loud noise ahead of me.
It got closer and closer,
It was my mum calling, 'Time for tea!'

Siân Priory (10)
St Joseph's RC Primary School, Burnham-on-Sea

OLLIE THE OCTOPUS

Ollie the octopus
Underneath the sea,
Looking, waiting for his tea.
Gives a little smile,
Then a little wink,
I hope he hasn't got his eye on me!

Briony Cooper (10)
St Joseph's RC Primary School, Burnham-on-Sea

THE BEACH

Seagulls on the wind soar,
I see their reflections on the water.
Underfoot is sand and estuary clay,
Muddy, squelchy, not with what we used to play.

Half submerged old bricks, caked in mortar,
Seaweed and driftwood litter the shore,
Never does the rhythm falter,
Delivered twice daily by marine lore.

Old gorse bushes with branches mangled,
Submit to the wind, their growth becomes angled.
The cheeky young grasses sway, duck and dive,
Avoiding the punch of the incoming tide.

End of day, time to go,
Sun is setting, light becomes low.
Islands silhouetted, a sight of great beauty,
Lighthouse winks to me, he's now on duty.

William Tasker (9)
St Joseph's RC Primary School, Burnham-on-Sea

THE APPLE PIE

Up above in the night sky
Falls down an apple pie.
It tastes so sweet,
Oh, what a treat.
It got burnt by the sun
And tastes like a bun.

Rebecca Pearce (9)
St Joseph's RC Primary School, Burnham-on-Sea

MY FAMILY

My family is always the same!

My little brother always has a runny nose,
My granddad calls me Ellie Rose.

My other brother's mad on Liverpool,
My sister thinks cats rule.

My granny wobbles her false teeth,
My sister has a boyfriend, Keith.

My nanny always gives us eggs,
My granddad detests clothes pegs.

Why can't they just be normal,
Like me?

Ellie Fry (9)
St Joseph's RC Primary School, Burnham-on-Sea

SOMETHING

There's something strange under my bed,
Something strange with a square-shaped head.
It snores loudly at night
And that is what gives me a fright.
At the back of my bed is a huge, big lump,
How that lump makes me jump!
That something is no fun,
But I'll tell you something,
If there's something under your bed,
Run!

Anna Beck (9)
St Joseph's RC Primary School, Burnham-on-Sea

READY-SALTED

Nothing else happened
That day.

Nothing much, anyway.

I got up, went to school,
Did the usual stuff.

Came home, watched telly,
Did the usual stuff.

Nothing else happened,
That day.

Nothing much, anyway.

But the eyeball in the crisps
Was enough.

Gregory Guyatt (9)
St Joseph's RC Primary School, Burnham-on-Sea

THE DOPEY SHEPHERD

There was a shepherd who had some sheep,
They were all so tired they fell asleep.
One was big, one was small,
The other one was *bigger* than them all.
He could not cope, but he was really a bit of a dope.
He washed really well, but without any soap.
There's one bit of advice,
Never trust a shepherd with some sheep,
They will probably fall asleep.

Caine Draper (10)
St Joseph's RC Primary School, Burnham-on-Sea

MY SISTER

My sister says she loves me,
She'll take me round the park,
She'll dresses me up in fancy clothes,
But that's just baby stuff!

My sister says she loves me,
She'll bunch my hair in tails,
We'll dance around in circles,
The world's a million sails,
But that's just baby stuff.

My sister says she loves me,
She'll buy me some ice cream.
We'll laugh and joke until we choke,
But that's still baby stuff!

Katherine Mckenzie (9)
St Joseph's RC Primary School, Burnham-on-Sea

ANIMALS' ARK

Leopards are spotty,
Either way they're still dotty.
Dolphins can always swim in the sea,
Fishes are good company.
Sighing is not a pig's hobby,
Rabbits' tails are always bobby.
Dogs like barking up the trees,
Sharks all swim in wavy seas.
Cats always purr away,
Lambs are born round about May.

Natasha Allen (10)
St Joseph's RC Primary School, Burnham-on-Sea

A TURTLE

Here is a turtle,
Bright as can be,
All different colours,
Dressed for tea.

A handsome chap he is indeed,
But unfortunately has only one speed.

Emma Shattock (10)
St Joseph's RC Primary School, Burnham-on-Sea

I AM

I am my mum's child,
I am a boy,
I am myself,
I am running,
I am eating,
I am jumping.

I am working,
I am writing,
I am cutting,
I am sticking,
I am smelling.

I am swimming,
I am splashing,
I am thinking,
I am playing,
I am looking.

I am Dean.

Dean Goldsmith (11)
Sedgemoor Manor Junior School

THE CAT

There was a cat on my bed.
A dog was outside barking.
The cat jumped off my bed.
Went out by the flat.

The cat went out.
There was a rat and a bat.
The bat was on the grass.
The rat was running around.

And the cat jumped on the bat.
And a hat fell on the fat rat.
Then we fell down,
And the bat sat on the rat.

Katie Lock (8)
Sedgemoor Manor Junior School

LOVE OTHERS

L   is for light that lights up your home.
O   is for open to open your heart.
V   is for violet that colours your world.
E   is for everlasting love.

O   is for others, that care
T   is for trust that you and I share
H   is for happiness I feel when with you
E   is for enjoying the things that we do
R   is for relationships, every need
S   is for sharing our love.

Abigail Brennan (9)
Sedgemoor Manor Junior School

THE START OF THE WEEK

Monday is the start of the week,
I wish it was not school.
At least we have got swimming,
So that's not bad at all.

Tuesday is the science day,
The brainiest day of my life.
Tuesday is my favourite day,
But don't stab me with that knife.

Wednesday is the music day,
The day I like to sing.
I sing and shout and scream
But you'd better join in.

Thursday is the art day,
The best day of my life,
I love to paint and sketch
And I try to do my best.

Friday is the last day,
Hip, hip, hooray!
I want to be the student of the week,
So hurry up and finish this day!

Mercedes Bowers (9)
Sedgemoor Manor Junior School

THE SPOOKY MONSTER

The spooky monster walks around at night
Waiting for his dinner
And a person went in,
And no one saw him again.

A witch went in
And she made some spooky friends.
They had a big, big spooky party,
And that's how it ends.

Danny Hemmings (8)
Sedgemoor Manor Junior School

YOUR SENSES

I can smell
lasagne cooking in the pan,
biscuits dipped into cups of tea,
food in the cupboard.

I can feel
biscuits crunching in my mouth,
lasagne running down my throat,
Cold apple juice sliding into my belly.

I can taste
hot beans that taste lovely,
cold lovely milk sliding into my belly,
noodles wiggling in my mouth.

I can see
trees waving in the wind,
the grass swaying as the wind goes by,
the leaves flying around the sky.

I can listen
to the crunching leaves as I step on them,
I can listen to the wind blowing and
the snow falling gently.

Tayia Jade Hiroz (8)
Sedgemoor Manor Junior School

DOWN IN THE CELLAR

Down in the cellar where nobody goes,
There's an old suitcase painted brown,
And in that, a puppet clown.
Up in the corner there is a spider spinning a web
And on the floor, there are broken broomsticks.
There is a ladder on the wall,
Pile of clothes on the floor with rats running around.

Adam Benner (9)
Sedgemoor Manor Junior School

GETTING UP

I heard my alarm clock go, ring, ring, ring.
I came down for breakfast, yum, yum, crunch.
I watch a bit of TV, blah, blah, blah and
Then I do my teeth, scrub, scrub, splash, splash, scrunch.
Then I go to school in the car, brum, brum, braa, braa.

Andrew Griffiths (9)
Sedgemoor Manor Junior School

CELLAR

Down in the cellar where nobody goes,
I saw a monster with a wiggly nose
And I didn't care if it touched me
Because it had no toes.

Reece Standerwick (10)
Sedgemoor Manor Junior School

THE MYSTERIOUS, FOGGY LAKE

One dark night on a mysterious, foggy lake,
There was a full moon.
It was like a UFO.
A little woman was carrying a miniature old stick,
The bridge was dark and spooky.
A frightening old tree was hanging down
Like there was a phantom hiding behind it.
A fish was jumping, like it was a spiky monster,
The lake was terrifyingly creepy.
The clouds went like they'd already done
Some shocking business.
It was foggy and the little woman was going fishing.
The cliffs in the background were foggy and mysterious.
You could smell smoke and dead leaves,
You could hear howling in the back ground,
From a werewolf on the top of a cliff.
The little woman went home with some fish.

Kimberley Thomas (8)
Sedgemoor Manor Junior School

WHAT A BUSY LIFE

I had breakfast, it went snap,
I stepped on a twig, it went crack.
I went to the zoo, heard a moo,
Playing with my friend, he shouted, 'Boo!'
In the summer, got stung by a buzzy buzz bee,
Going down the slide screaming, 'Whee, whee, whee.'
Going to my dad's, heard thunder crash,
Banging on the drums, they went bash.

Nick Phillips (10)
Sedgemoor Manor Junior School

THE ABANDONED BRIDGE

One dark night by a dark, dark bridge,
There was a phantom figure
Under a shiny moon like a silver coin.

Who could be out on a night
When the tree looks like a monster
By the abandoned bridge?

Nobody would go out
When the sharks could leap out at you,
A ghostly hand could reach out of the tree,
A hooded ghost with a scythe could come out,
An image of a man fading into a skeleton in a hood.

If the griffin might come out
And crush the bones of anything in its path,
In the haunted forest, the griffin might fly away.

The abandoned bridge would be haunted
By the man who could be drowned
By the river, under the shiny moon like a silver coin.

Adam Busby (9)
Sedgemoor Manor Junior School

PEACEFUL

Peaceful is the colour of a red school jumper.
It smells like roses on a rose bush,
It tastes like banana ice cream,
It sounds like Death of Peace,
It feels like somebody's furry teddy bear,
It lives in a house of peace.

Jodie Williams (10)
Sedgemoor Manor Junior School

ONE DARK NIGHT

One dark night, in the harbour of the city,
A flame was burning.
It got bigger and bigger,
Sparks flew off.

Some big ships were in the sea,
The waves splashed about.
The small moon was above the sea.

The rough sea was dangerous,
It was a bad storm.
The wind was roaring,
The waves crashed against the wall.

Dark clouds surrounded the area,
The fire spread across the land.
People waited and waited
For the ships to set sail.

Emily Ives (8)
Sedgemoor Manor Junior School

GETTING UP

When I hear my mum shout, 'Get up,'
I say, 'In a minute.'
So then I get up and get dressed for school,
Then I have my breakfast,
Yum, yum, crunch, crunch.
Then we get in the car and my mum starts the car,
Brum, brum, screech.

Joshua Baker (9)
Sedgemoor Manor Junior School

THE GLOOMY HALL

One dark night
In a dark, dark hall,
Stood a dark, dark knight
In a dark, dark suit.

The walls were dirty,
The knight was black,
The place was gloomy,
The rooms were dark.

I looked at the knight
In the dark, dark suit.
The suit was black
And his eyes were red.

I looked at the walls,
I looked in the rooms,
The rooms were clean,
But the walls were dirty
In that gloomy place.

Conner Hillman (9)
Sedgemoor Manor Junior School

A DARK NIGHT

One dark, cloudy, wet night in a busy little town,
The lights were dim and the people were out,
The people were out and about.
The town was damp and the huge shop was crowded
With hundreds of people.
The shops were full, kids and adults
Have loads of food and toys for the children.

Becky Rowley (8)
Sedgemoor Manor Junior School

THE CITY HARBOUR

One dark night
On the moonlit city harbour,
People watched the hot, sparkling flames
On the sea wall.

The sailing ships crashed
Against the sea walls fiercely.
They fought their way
Through the crashing waves.

The flames were as hot as blazes,
The people screamed in terror
While the waves crashed
Against the sea wall.

Holly Miller (8)
Sedgemoor Manor Junior School

SPACE

Space is dark,
Space sparkles day and night,
Space is big.
Planets surround space and new life is born.
Plants live on planets and hate the dark night.
At night you can see space and planets.
Spaces is big,
Space is 2.225 thousand light years big.
Space is sometimes hot.
Space has light such as the sun and moon.
Space is beautiful.

Christopher Thomas (11)
Sedgemoor Manor Junior School

KIDS

Sit up straight
Said Mum to Matt,
Keep your cat
Off the mat.
Do not eat meat
Off a seat,
Your mouth is full,
Don't talk to Pete.
Keep your mouth shut
When you eat,
Keep still or you'll
Fall off your seat.
If you want cheese,
You will say please.
Don't climb trees
That will scrape your knees.
If then we kids
Cause such a fuss,
Why do you go on
Having us?

Zoe Harris (9)
Sedgemoor Manor Junior School

THE STRANGE MAN

There was a man who was a nutter,
Who made a fuss over butter.
He went to the shops,
Bought a bottle of pop
And ended up in the gutter.

Kyle Frost (10)
Sedgemoor Manor Junior School

KIDS

Sit up straight,
Said Mum to Scott,
Keep your hands
Off the cot.
Do not eat bread
Off a bed.
Your mouth is full,
Don't shout at Fred.
Keep your mouth shut
When you eat,
Keep still or you'll
Fall off your seat.
If you want cheese,
You will say please.
Don't play with me,
That will tease
If then we kids
Cause such a fuss,
Why do you go on
Having us?

Rachel Selway (10)
Sedgemoor Manor Junior School

TORNADO

I spin like a coin
Tossed in the air.
I take sheep and cows
From the ground.
I make the world roar,
Like a dinosaur.

Dominic Best (10)
Sedgemoor Manor Junior School

MY CAT

I have a small cat called Little Puss
Who is always messing about
She hides in the car, hides in my room
And won't come out when I shout

She is furry, fat and stripy
Quite normal for a cat
But gets stuck in the cat flap
When trying to chase a rat

I love my cat, Little Puss
Even though she is very silly
I know she loves me back
Because she purrs when she is with me.

Jennifer Prowse (9)
Sedgemoor Manor Junior School

MY PET

My pet
is
kind to
me
but when
he
bites,
it hurts
so very
much.

Lauren Howe (8)
Sedgemoor Manor Junior School

WHAT IF?

What if the world ended?
Would we have evolved,
Would we be robots,
Would the world ever become again,
Would we feel it,
Would we suddenly disappear or
Would we slowly disintegrate in space?
Would the world suddenly explode in one,
Would it start crumbling away?
What if the world ended?

If we didn't disintegrate and we stayed whole,
Would we travel through black holes
And into another universe?
Would we travel through magnetic storms,
Would we finally be able to touch the stars,
Would we burn if we got too close to the sun,
Would we survive or would our heads explode?
What if the world ended?

Kirsty Newman (10)
Sedgemoor Manor Junior School

ANGER

Anger is like a deep, deep black.
Anger feels like the heat of a fire inside you.
Anger is like a gorilla's hands
When it travels through the jungle
Anger looks like the heat of a heatwave.
It makes me feel wound up inside.

Ryan Daly (9)
Sedgemoor Manor Junior School

THE FREAKY FROG AND SCARED DOG

At night, Freaky Frog comes out,
He scares the scared dog,
But when the dog goes bark,
The Freaky Frog jumps away in the dark.

When the master come down,
He pulls a nasty frown.
Always he hears a bark in the dark,
But when the master calls 'Mrack'
The frog jumps away in the dark.

So when the frog goes back,
The witch attacks.
Now it's no more a pack,
Because he got sent back.

Jodi Searle (8)
Sedgemoor Manor Junior School

HAPPINESS THEN SADNESS

You are full of happiness.
Sometimes you feel sad and lonely,
But don't let that spoil your happiness inside.
When you are sad, you just want to be left alone
And it might make you feel much better.
Happy then sad, it is better
To be sad then to be happy.
Sadness is like a falling star.
Happiness is like a shooting star.

Natasha Baker (10)
Sedgemoor Manor Junior School

TWINKLE, TWINKLE

Twinkle, twinkle, little bat,
How I wonder where you're at.
Up above the world so high,
Like a tea tray in the sky.

Twinkle, twinkle, hear the dormouse
Singing in its sleep.
Twinkle, twinkle, twinkle,
They have to pinch him to make him stop.

When he woke up, they all said 'boo!'
The dormouse said, 'What are you doing?'
They all said, 'We had to pinch you to make you stop singing,
Twinkle, Twinkle, in your sleep.'

Jade Williams (9)
Sedgemoor Manor Junior School

YELLOW

Yellow is a submarine,
Yellow is a shining beach,
Yellow is a merit,
Yellow is a demerit.

Yellow is a good thing,
Yellow is a car,
Yellow is shells like glittering stars!

Yellow is a butterfly,
Yellow is some butter,
Yellow are our English books and
Yellow is a cone.

Ashlee Rawles (8)
Sedgemoor Manor Junior School

MY POEM

I like the feel of
my soft teddy bear as I cuddle him
bubbly shampoo in my hair
my blue, furry book.

I like the taste of
bubbly chocolate in my mouth
minty toothpaste as I'm brushing my teeth
squashy tomatoes as I'm eating them with my teeth.

I like the sound of
drums being banged with the loud stick
vegetables crunching on my plate
wind blowing up in the sky.

I like the smell of
fish and chips cooking in the oven
hot roast potatoes
body spray as my dad puts it on him.

I like the sight of
birds singing in the trees
my dog running after the ball
squirrels climbing up the trees to find some nuts.

Larissa Turner (8)
Sedgemoor Manor Junior School

MONSTERS

Monsters are scary
Monsters are bad
Monsters are hairy
Monsters are sad

They eat you up
Each little bone
And when you get in
You're not alone . . .

Leanne Marie Hale (10)
Sedgemoor Manor Junior School

SENSES POEM

I like the taste of
a big, juicy apple at home time.
A crunchy Christmas pudding for my afters.
Ice-cold ice cream sliding down my throat.

I like to listen to
the lightning thumping all over the house.
Buzzing bumblebees crunching on leaves.
The wind blowing the trees.

I like the feel of
silk swaying on my face.
Shampoo bubbling on my hair.
Hot chocolate and biscuits filling my belly.
A bump wheel on a motorbike.

I like to watch
the rain splashing in puddles.
The fire flickering at people.
The birds flying over me.
Rain coming down from the clouds.

I like to smell
My mum's perfume spraying in the air.
Mum's dinner cooking and sniffing the air.

Gemma Wood (7)
Sedgemoor Manor Junior School

MY SENSES

I like the taste of
brown, toasty bread,
dunking biscuits in cups of tea,
strawberry sugary doughnuts.

I like the feel of
snapping photos,
burning hot shells on a boiled egg,
soft silky plants.

I like the sound of
smashing, loud music,
banging, yellow thunder.

I like the smell of
burnt toast,
soft chocolate spread sandwiches.

I like to watch
a dog play with his bone,
watch TV
the powerful lightning striking
down to the patio.

Charlie Oram (7)
Sedgemoor Manor Junior School

THE WINDY NIGHT

One dark night, as the wind blew
And the fire glowed and crackled,
Dark figures all crowded around
To see people sailing off on their old, wooden boats.

As the sea crashed
Against the old, crooked walls,
The figures all watched in astonishment,
But no one knew what would happen to the poor sailors.

Abby Mitchell (8)
Sedgemoor Manor Junior School

SENSES

I like the smell of burgers on the cooker
and cakes with strawberries on top
and the smell of smelly pens

I like the taste of
mint sauce on meat
ham sandwiches
and Coco Pops and potatoes

I like to listen to
cars going down the motorway
and drums making a noise
and the PC with the volume up

I like the feel of ice cubes and
my teddy's and parrot's tail
and a drill vibrating

I like to watch the aeroplanes
and animals
and television
and birds.

Marcus Bell (8)
Sedgemoor Manor Junior School

SENSES POEM

I like the taste of
Juicy grapes,
Crumbling, creamy strawberries,
Crunchy carrots,
Cold ice cream running down my throat.

I like the feel of
Silky feathers tickling my face,
Soft smooth skin of a baby.

I like the sound of
Seagulls squawking in the sky,
Birds singing in the trees,
Popcorn sizzling in the frying pan,
Eggs as birds hatch.

I like to watch
Birds flapping in the sky,
Snow falling from the bright blue sky.

Paige Stacey (7)
Sedgemoor Manor Junior School

THE CATS

There are two cats that sit on mats
And like to wear caps.
Every night when the light has gone
They go hunting for gold,
Then bring it back home.

Christopher Winn (8)
Sedgemoor Manor Junior School

I COULD

I could wash my dog and wipe him dry
And then go and look at the sky,

Give him food and water too
And then put him in bed fast asleep with you,

And in the morning, he will bark
For his food in the dark,

And at night he will bark
For his food, in the dark

And then I will go and call
For Katie and Clark,

And all these things and many more,
I'll do tomorrow, that's for sure.

Holly Ingram (8)
Sedgemoor Manor Junior School

GLOOMY NIGHT

One gloomy Sunday night,
I can see a dark shadow
Down a dull street,
Staring at me, staring at me?
What could it be, what is it, what is it?
The wind is blowing,
The lights are flashing.
Is it a UFO, is it an ogre?
Nobody knows.
It's coming closer, closer, closer!

Kirsty James (9)
Sedgemoor Manor Junior School

ONE SPARKLING NIGHT

One sparkling night
In a little gloomy village,
It was very wet and slippery,
The clouds were floating slowly,
The moon shone brightly
In the misty, green sky,
A very tall church stood.
The moon was above the dark church.
The galloping horse rushed by
With a dark figure on its back.
The ground was shining.
I wonder why?

Jasmine Lewis (9)
Sedgemoor Manor Junior School

SCHOOL TIME

I like school,
I go to the pool
With my school,
I play in the playground
And have some fun.
My teacher teaches me
Things to do
And I do them all too.
I have some lunch
And eat it all
And sometimes I leave
A bit of it.

Mena Hajar (8)
Sedgemoor Manor Junior School

ONE DARK NIGHT

One dark night in a deep, dark forest
Stood an abandoned house.
A mysteriously blurred, hooded shadow
Came galloping by.
As the horse was on its way to the abandoned house,
He stood waiting. As he was waiting, he heard a noise,
He had a look to find out what it was.
A blue-hooded man came and scared him,
He charged after him.
When he went through the leaves, they rustled,
Then he went.

T-Anna Buxton (9)
Sedgemoor Manor Junior School

SOMETHING OR SOMEONE

One dark night when the full moon was out,
A man or woman, something, was over there.
The clouds were there in the air,
The moon shone on the water,
Suddenly there was a big howl.
A whatever-it-is was moving in the darkness.
In the distance, there was a ray of light,
Flashing on and off.
Just then, the ground shook,
Then the bridge collapsed.
The thing got in.

Brett Collins (9)
Sedgemoor Manor Junior School

THE WIZARD'S SPELL OF MYSTERIES

A wizard had spells like mysteries of the greatest
And he liked to make mysteries and all the people liked his mysteries,
But they also fled his accidents.

The thing was, he sometimes tells the people with no spells
And that means they can get past the non-magic places
And in the spell-binding places.

They can get spell books and get a broomstick
And get back to the non-magic places.

One day the wizard can make every mystery
And they can work for every day,
But one day he can do it.

Matthew Williams (8)
Sedgemoor Manor Junior School

HOLIDAY SITES

H   olidays are fun,
O   n the hot, sunny beach,
L   iving your lifetime,
I   love the breezes,
D   on't like the coldness,
A   nd I love the food.
Y   es, you should come.

S   ites you stay on,
I   t's a wonderful view,
T   ime to go and shop for clothes.
E   asy to find your way around,
S   o small as Bridgewater.

Gary Agnew (11)
Sedgemoor Manor Junior School

COLOURS

Black bird,
White snow,
Mellow yellow,
Sunny sunflower,
Green grass,
Blue bluebells,
Golden garden,
Silver sand,
Red roses,
Purple violets,
Black, white, green and yellow,
All the colours in the world,
Together.

Jade Roberts (7)
Sedgemoor Manor Junior School

THE BIRD AND THE OWL

One dull night in the middle of the town,
I was running to the church in a panic,
Then all of a sudden I saw a mysterious owl.
The owl hooted all night and
Stared at me all day with red eyes,
And all of a sudden, a bird of prey killed the owl.
The bird was black and grey.
The bird's owner was a captain of the pirates
And he owned several boats,
Which was very rare for a man of his age,
His age was ninety-eight.

Hayley Moule (8)
Sedgemoor Manor Junior School

SENSES POEM

I like the taste of
a crunchy juicy apple at home.
Some crumbly brown bread for my lunch.
Some fresh, sticky sweets in a bag.
A cup of hot chocolate.

I like to listen to
a buzzing bumblebee in the sky.
Seagulls squeaking in the sun.
Aeroplanes flying past me.

I like the feel of
smooth, silky silk in the shops.
A bumpy wheel of a motorbike.
Hard solid metal on a car.
Fluffy feathers on a bird.

I like to watch
birds flying over the hills.
The snow melting around me.
The sun glowing in the sky.
The rain hammering from the clouds.

Lloyd Hooper (7)
Sedgemoor Manor Junior School

THE OGRE

An ogre was in my bed,
An ogre was in my wardrobe,
An ogre was on my computer,
An ogre was watching my TV,
An ogre was putting on my clothes,
There's an ogre in my bedroom.

Stephen Cross (8)
Sedgemoor Manor Junior School

SCHOOL

School is fun,
School is cool,
School is happy,
And that's not all.

School is funny,
School's a ball,
School is healthy,
And that's not all.

School is learning,
What to do,
And when you learn . . .
            clever you!

Sandra Boulton (9)
Sedgemoor Manor Junior School

MY VALENTINE'S POEM

Roses are red, violets are blue
You love me and I love you
I love you, I love you
With all my heart
I pray each night we never part!
You make me happy, you make me sad
You are mine and I'm so glad
You're on my mind, day and night
That's how I know our love is right!
Just remember what I say
'I love you more and more each day.'

Gavin Smith (8)
Sedgemoor Manor Junior School

MY FIVE SENSES

I like the taste of
my nan's tasty roast dinner
my mum's warm hot chocolate
and warm biscuits with chocolate bits
my dad's cottage pie.

I like the feel of
a soft wet wipe on my skin
my feet being tickled by
a lovely feather on my skin.

I like the smell of
my nan's green paint on her wallpaper

I like to watch
Power Puff Girls on the TV
on the cosy sofa
My kittens playing with their mouse.

I like the sound of
birds singing on a tree
the lovely sound of my cat's purring.

Stacey Mirto (7)
Sedgemoor Manor Junior School

CUCUMBER

I am nice and juicy,
I am nice and fine,
I am nice and green,
I am nice with tomatoes,
I am nice on toast,
I am nice in a sandwich.

James Taylor (10)
Sedgemoor Manor Junior School

My Poem

I like the feel of
my soft cuddly teddy bear
to cuddle at night-time.

I like the taste of
apple juice going down my throat
and crunchy bread in my mouth.

I like the sound of
the drums being banged with the noisy stick
and the rain going drip, drip, on my window.

I like the smell of
roast dinner in the cooking pan
the soap in the bathroom
and roast potatoes in the oven.

I like to watch
the birds flying in the sky
my dog running around
me going mad at a butterfly swinging in a tree.

Mikki Hole (7)
Sedgemoor Manor Junior School

Mr Wizard

'Mr Wizard, Mr Wizard,
Do you have freaky shoes?'
'Yes I do have freaky shoes.'
'And do you have a spiky hat?'
'Yes I do!'
'And do you have a freaky face?'

Ashley Mills (8)
Sedgemoor Manor Junior School

MY SENSES POEM

I like the taste of
marmalade on crumpets
Jammy Dodgers with a glass of icy Coke
Red, juicy strawberries.

I like the smell of
My Auntie Val's pink, beautiful perfume
That she gave me.

I like the sound of the TV.

I like the feel of sunflowers.

I like the sight of ghosts in my bedroom
I like to watch the birds sing from out my window
I like the smell of hot dogs
I like the feel of my bath.

Rebecca Addicott (7)
Sedgemoor Manor Junior School

IN THE DEEP, DARK FOREST

One spooky dark night in a dim forest not far away from here,
Stood an elderly old house with lots and lots of things around it.
Then a galloping, hooded shadow came out of nowhere,
A glowing light is behind a tree. The light is greeny-blue.
I think a phantom is there, all I could hear was click-clap,
I couldn't hear anything except that.
The night has begun and it's just getting worse,
My temperature is rising, I am getting scared.

Marissa O'Neill (9)
Sedgemoor Manor Junior School

THE SILENT MOUNTAIN

From the mountain to the sea, there's a silent sound,
Shadowy figures creeping around,
In and out of the houses they go.

In the air there's a funny smell, the smell that smells like acid.
Where is the smell coming from?
High on the mountain top.

So the figures sailed away in a boat like a raft,
A very cold draught filled the air.
By now it was night and twinkling light
Of the stars in the sky.

Stephanie Nichols (9)
Sedgemoor Manor Junior School

MY SENSES

I like the taste of my mum's burning hot sausages.
I like the taste of ice cream and jelly with chocolate custard.
I like to feel the lumpy popcorn popping up and down.
I like to hear the thunder and lightning in the gentle drops of rain.
I like to see my mum cooking sausages with beans.
I like the smell of hot chocolate with chocolate cream on top.
I like the smell of chocolate cake with custard.
I like the smell of sizzling sausages in a burning hot pan.
I like to see tasty hot chocolate.
I like the taste of lovely, burning hot pizza.
I like to hear my dad's car go *Brmmm, brmmm!*

Ryan Millis (8)
Sedgemoor Manor Junior School

OUR FIVE SENSES

I like the taste of
milky cereal in the bright morning
hot chocolate in the cold winter
sweet biscuits in a hot cup of tea on a dark night.

I like the feel of
cold, freezing water
boiling hot water
soft, squashy Playdoh.

I like the smell of
soft, sweet bubblegum
soft fairy cakes
smooth cups.

I like to watch
my black, big dog jumping in the park
my baby brother crawling on the shining floor
my dad playing on the Game Boy.

I like to listen
to birds chirping in the swinging trees
music singing in my ear
beautiful goldfish swimming beautifully in their tank
my dog barking madly at night.

Mason Galloway (7)
Sedgemoor Manor Junior School

SUMMER

Summer is the best time of the year.
Summer is hot.
Sometimes we have beer
Sometimes my dad cleans a lot.

Sometimes it is very bright
Sometimes it is very cool
Sometimes it is light
Sometimes we have chocolate.

Jessica Woollan (9)
Sedgemoor Manor Junior School

MY SENSES

I like the taste of
tasty hot chocolate at night.
Sweet taste of bananas.
A big bunch of juicy grapes.
Hot crumpets or toast.

I like the feel of
cold iced water in the hot sun.
A small baby's soft skin.
The sand as I run along the beach.

I like to listen to
birds tweeting on a winter day.
Music against the door.
Birds singing in the trees.

I like to watch
the tweeting birds in the bright sky.
Trees swaying from side to side.
Plants growing in the sun.

I like the smell of
plants in the warm sun.
Autumn trees in the bright sky.
Smelly pens on my pieces of paper.

Shelley Hooper (7)
Sedgemoor Manor Junior School

MY SENSES

I like the sound of
popcorn popping out of the pan
Mum shouting us for our dinner
Dad driving home from smelly work.

I like the smell of
my new snuggly quilt on my bed
Mum cooking delicious lovely dinner
Dad making yummy and delicious cakes.

I like to watch
my mum making my cosy warm bed
and me watching TV all day on the cosy sofa
Dad doing painting on the wallpaper

I like the feel of
the middle part of a sunflower with all the
bumpy seeds in the middle
bumpy seeds of the beautiful sunflower.

I like the taste of
Dad making delicious cookies
and Mum making yummy dinner.

Jessica Bowers (8)
Sedgemoor Manor Junior School

SOMEBODY STOLE MY PANTS

Somebody stole my pants,
When I went to France,
'Oh no,' I said,
When I went to bed,
'It has to be one of my aunts.'

Ashley Scott (10)
Sedgemoor Manor Junior School

SENSES

I like the taste of juicy apples and big, long bananas,
hot chocolate and ice cream at home.
I like the feel of a big teddy bear,
a big, soft ball,
I like to watch the birds singing up high in the tree,
the fire burning to keep me warm,
and the sparkling sunshine.

I like to listen to the fire crackling and
the popcorn popping in the pan,
I like the smell of strawberry soap in my bath,
minty toothpaste,
and roses in the summer.

Lewis Eichmann (8)
Sedgemoor Manor Junior School

SAUSAGES SIZZLING IN A PAN

Five big sausages sitting in a pan, one went, bang,
then there were four.
Four big sausages sitting in a pan, one went pop,
then there were three.
Three big sausages sitting in a pan, Mum ate one,
then there were two.
Two big sausages sitting in a pan. Dad ate one,
then there was one.
One big sausage sitting in a pan, one went crash....
then there were none.

Adam Howe (8)
Sedgemoor Manor Junior School

I KNOW A WITCH

I know a witch.
She lives in a ditch
At the very old farm.
When she wakes up
She makes a spell
To make everyone smell.

When she has finished
Then she goes back to sleep.
Then we go to the magic sheep.
And he says 'Go to the witch and say
'Wake up you bad thing, because
I will break your bad ring.'

'No, no,' the witch says,
'You will never break it.'
'Yes I will.'

Ellie May (9)
Sedgemoor Manor Junior School

WATER

Water is calm,
Water can be dangerous,
Water can be fun.
Water cannot be fun,
Water can be cold,
Water can be hot,
Water can be dirty,
Water can be clean.

Sam Saunders (10)
Sedgemoor Manor Junior School

WALKING THROUGH THE PARK

One wet night I was walking through the park.
One wet night it was very, very dark.
So I walked on and I heard a noise behind me.
I turned round to see.

There stood a man as tall as me.
He had long teeth
And green eyes
And a knife to stab me.

I ran away to the shop.
And the man said 'Hey you, stop.'
So I ran home,
As fast as could be.

My dad came out, he would save me.

Sam Facey (8)
Sedgemoor Manor Junior School

MONKEY

Monkey, monkey, in the tree,
Swinging from side to side.
People come, why hide?
Monkey, monkey, in the sky,
Why look so sad
And serious and mad?
Monkey, monkey, swinging ropes,
Upside down, don't lose your hopes.
Monkey, monkey, try to escape,
Please . . .

Jayne Tucker (9)
Sedgemoor Manor Junior School

FRIENDS!

F   is for friendly!
    Give me an F!

R   is for reliable!
    Give me an R!

I   is for interesting!
    Give me an I!

E   is for enjoyment!
    Give me an E!

N   is for nice!
    Give me an N!

D   is for dearest!
    Give me a D!

S   is for special!
    Give me an S!

What does it spell?

Friends!

Stacey Hurley (10)
Sedgemoor Manor Junior School

THE FOOTBALL POEM

Football's fun,
Football's good,
To play it is good,
To win it is good,
To win the final cup.

Jamie Pike (7)
Sedgemoor Manor Junior School

HOSPITALS!

I'm going to the hospital,
I've just been sick,
I'm really, really happy
because school I can skip.
I'm reading my book,
because it's about a crook.
I'm lying in bed,
with my sleepy head.
I'm sitting on the chair
with long black hair.
I am falling asleep,
with not a peep.
I drank my drink,
and I spilt it in the sink.
I ate my dinner,
and am still getting thinner.
I fell out of my bed,
and hit my head.
I got back in,
and whacked my chin.

Kirsty Hole (10)
Sedgemoor Manor Junior School

A MUMMY FROM EGYPT

A mummy from Egypt is mean.
A mummy from Egypt is keen.
A mummy from Egypt is hungry.
A mummy from Egypt is scary.

Liam Cornell (7)
Sedgemoor Manor Junior School

EVERYBODY RAP

Everybody rap
Everybody rap
Can you do a rap?
Can you do a rap?
Can you make a word?
Can you make a word?

I like to rap
So everybody rap
Rap, rap, rap,
Everybody rap.

Black and white are all the same
So make a rap and rap, rap, rap.

Sarah Hutt (9)
Sedgemoor Manor Junior School

SCHOOL DAYS

Mondays, it is time for school
When I get home I go in my pool.

Tuesdays are horrible days
All I want to do is play.

Wednesdays, it always rains
It's the day when I'm a pain.

Thursdays, only two days to go
Although there's still Friday.

Fridays, it's the end of the week
Now I'm gonna go to sleep.

Jodie Jodkowski (9)
Sedgemoor Manor Junior School

KIDS

'Sit up straight!'
said Mum to Ted.
Keep your toys off the bed.
Do not eat meat
off a spoon.
Your mouth is full -
don't go to the moon.
Keep your mouth shut
when you eat.
Keep still or you'll
fall off your seat.
If you want more
you will say 'Please.'
Don't play with
those dirty fleas.'
If then we kids
cause such a fuss,
why do you go on
having us?

Liam Pope (10)
Sedgemoor Manor Junior School

ANGER

Anger is red
It smells like a red-hot bubbling cauldron
Anger tastes like red burning poison
It sounds like scary angry music
It feels like a red-hot boiling fire
Anger lives on the Devil's side.

Amy Leitch (9)
Sedgemoor Manor Junior School

KIDS

'Sit up straight,'
said Mum to Mat
'keep your hands
off the cat.
Do not eat meat
off a seat.
Your mouth is full
don't try to speak.
Keep your mouth shut
when you eat
keep still or you'll
fall off your seat.
If you want some yellow cheese
you will say, 'Please, please, please.'
Don't touch my knees
that will make me sneeze.'
If then we kids
cause such a fuss,
why do you go on
having us?

Matthew Entwistle (10)
Sedgemoor Manor Junior School

FIRE

The fire rages like a thunderstorm.
It will burn your skin,
So do not touch it, it will kill you
And your house and your pets.
So keep away from fire,
It takes your life from you.
Be careful.

Tanya Varnam (11)
Sedgemoor Manor Junior School

KIDS

'Sit up straight,'
said Mum to Fred.
'Keep your hands
off the bread.
Eat your veg.
Eat your greens.
Keep your
hands off your beans.
Brush your teeth
every day
otherwise they will
fade away.'
If then we kids
cause you strain
why don't you
put me in pain?

Andrew Rees Peacey (10)
Sedgemoor Manor Junior School

FIRE

Fire is like a burning pain
Destroying everything in its path.
It does not stop without a fight,
But when it's gone it can still come back.
Beware of fire, it can kill you, burn you,
So beware of fire that looms through the night and day,
Never stopping for a drink.
It will laugh at pain and suffering,
That's fire.

Chris Power (10)
Sedgemoor Manor Junior School

THE FROG

Once there was a frog.
He lived in a ditch near some fog.
He was called Hopper Frog.
I live in a hole.
My friend is a mole.
The frog hopped into the forest.
He found a slice of pork.
He had quite a talk.
The frog found plenty of other stuff
Somewhere rough.
When the frog went home,
He found his friend Mole.
Of course he was in his hole.
When the frog got in he found a . . .
Chair, brand new, which made the
Frog so happy and a bit nappy.

Marcus Keen (9)
Sedgemoor Manor Junior School

ELLIE BELLY JELLY

Ellie Belly is so smelly,
She lives in the bottom of a well.
She's made of jelly.
All she does is eat jelly
And play with jelly all day.
She never eats well,
All day long she eats jelly.

Ashley Addicott (9)
Sedgemoor Manor Junior School

FEELINGS

Love is red like roses,
Love is also pink,
Love tastes like it's candyfloss,
It really makes you think.

Anger's like fire,
Burning in your heart,
But as you surely know now,
It's a very special part.

Happiness is jolly,
A friendly sort of thing,
A sort of glow inside you,
Happiness will bring.

Joy is blue like Heaven,
Dancing on a star,
Joy will make you happy,
A feeling that goes far.

Charlotte Constable (9)
Sedgemoor Manor Junior School

MY DOG

My dog is mad,
My dog is sad,
My dog is bad,
But he's the best I've ever had.
His coat is rough,
He's very tough,
But he's the best I've ever had.

Lauren Huxtable (8)
Sedgemoor Manor Junior School

MY DOG CRACKER

My dog is funny,
My dog is silly,
My dog is cute and cuddly.
My dog is small,
My dog is brown,
My dog eats a lot.
My dog is brave,
My dog is strange,
My dog is a fast runner.

Rosie Keirle (7)
Sedgemoor Manor Junior School

A DARK NIGHT

Once, fifteen people were about on a black, wet night.
It was a nasty scene, people were soggy and wet
Because it was slightly greasy, slippery and to me
It spoiled the evening.
The path was black and grey and also soggy.
The moon was shining brightly,
The lights were on quietly.

Amber Baker (8)
Sedgemoor Manor Junior School

MY FAMILY

I am writing this poem,
while I am still rowing,
my nan is still sewing,
and my brother's still growing.

My sister has got blisters,
and my mother hasn't kissed her,
and my dad looks familiar,
because he looks like my sister.

Dean Mills (11)
Sedgemoor Manor Junior School

THIS LITTLE PIG

This little pig had money.
This little pig was funny.
This little pig was mad.
This little pig was sad.
And . . .
This little pig went 'Wee'
All in the poem book.

Stephen Blake (10)
Sedgemoor Manor Junior School

TEACHERS

Teachers scream,
teachers shout,
teachers try to boss us about.
Children screaming and shouting
running around endless corridors.
Slipping over slippery floors
banging into hard doors.

Sarah Collins (10)
Sedgemoor Manor Junior School

DENTIST

I'm going to the dentist's
I'm shaking like mad
I'm going to the dentist's
What could be as bad?

I'm in the dentist's waiting room
I'm as scared as scared can be
I'm in the dentist's waiting room
I hope I can eat my tea!

I'm sitting in the chair
I'm going up, down and back
I'm sitting in the chair
Oh I wish he'd get the sack!

I'm lying in the chair
He's turned on his little light
I'm lying down in the chair
He's given me such a fright!

I'm coming back up
What does he think?
I'm coming back up
I've been sick in the sink!

I'm out the chair
I'm out the door
I'm out the chair
Only six months more!

Hannah Whitehouse (9)
Sedgemoor Manor Junior School

AMAZEMENT

As the waves crash against the rocks
the sailors watch in amazement as
a fire erupts in the still shivering town as the
waves crash up against the galleon.
The sailors are scared and aware of what could happen.

It is as if killer whales are crashing up against
the enemy in a desperate fight for prey.
The sailors' loved ones watch in sadness,
afraid of the killer whales' capabilities.
Could it crash? Could it crumble?
No one knows as they watch in amazement.

The waves still crashing and the fire still erupting.
Somebody's screaming, no one knows as
they watch in amazement.

The moonlight is shining, the stars are glowing
The universe is looking down on the killer whales'
desperate fight for prey. No one knows
as they watch in amazement.

The storm is over, the lightning has stopped striking.
Everyone knows as they *watch in relief.*

Joshua Godfrey (9)
Sedgemoor Manor Junior School

THE CAT

The cat sat on a mat eating biscuits away.
Along came a dog who gave her a shock
And they were drinking cider all day.

Susan Gardner (10)
Sedgemoor Manor Junior School

SEASONS

Summer is good,
Summer is good,
But in winter
You need a hood.

Winter is bad,
Winter is bad,
Because in summer
I'm glad.

Spring leaves puddles
Spring leaves puddles.

I'm good in autumn
My mum gives me cuddles.

Autumn leaves sail,
Autumn leaves sail,
So in spring
I walk on the wall.

Nathan Mitchell (8)
Sedgemoor Manor Junior School

BEING KIRSTY

K   is for Kicking babe,
I   is for Ice cream,
R   is for Rosebush,
S   is for Super chick,
T   is for Talking,
Y   is for Yellow, the colour of my face.

Kirsty means 'happy and smiley.'

Kirsty Lilley (10)
Sedgemoor Manor Junior School

HIDDEN TREASURE

Down at the bottom of the sea
Wildlife is all I can see
The fish are red
Swimming along the seabed
There are slimy black eels
Polluted with wheels
Crabs and jellyfish
What a wish
Swimming is leisure
Look, I've found some treasure.
I've seen a lot of nature
What a cool adventure.

Sam Godfrey (11)
Sedgemoor Manor Junior School

DEAD OF THE NIGHT

One dark night at a mysterious lake
Stood a ghost on the moor,
Looking up at the creepy sky above,
Like a black poltergeist looking for trouble.
The moon looking like a five-pence piece,
Fishes jumping like sharks,
The scary bridge with monsters
With eyes like car lights,
Waiting to kill someone
In the dead of the night.

Johno Speed (9)
Sedgemoor Manor Junior School

ABOUT A GIRAFFE

Giraffes have spots
giraffes have long necks and they're tall
they have long legs
they have long tails
and two big ears
giraffes eat leaves
giraffes can see anything from a mile
and they have big eyes
I've never seen one before
because giraffes live in Australia
and I live in Bridgwater, Somerset
and Bridgwater hasn't got any jungles.
So the giraffes will have to stay in the zoo
and the giraffes will not like that because
they will be with all the spiteful animals.

Damian Brown (8)
Sedgemoor Manor Junior School

SADNESS

Sadness is a falling tear,
A broken heart,
Deep regret,
Near to the bottom,
Everlasting pain,
Sadness is a cloudy sky,
Sadness is a heart to die.

Kirstin Trunks (11)
Sedgemoor Manor Junior School

FIRE BEGAN

It took the spines from a hedgehog,
The heat from the sun.
It took its colour from blood,
The danger from a shark.
It took its speed from a cheetah,
The smoke from burnt toast.

Fire was made!

Orion Draper (10)
Sedgemoor Manor Junior School

WHAT IF?

What if there were no people walking down the street?
What if there were no children playing happily?
What if there were no cars zooming down the road?
What if there were no noise?
What if there were nothing?
It would be called the world with nothing.

Kerry Mills (11)
Sedgemoor Manor Junior School

LOVE

Love is pink like candyfloss,
Love smells like roses on Mother's Day,
Love tastes like hot fudge cake on a cold night,
Love feels like a fluffy teddy bear in your bed,
Love lives in Heaven where the angels sing.

Jennifer Parsons (9)
Sedgemoor Manor Junior School

CARNIVAL

C lubs are busy making floats all year
A ll the music going through your cold ears
R ed, orange and yellow, all the tropical colours they pick
N ow everyone is trying on their costumes making sure they fit
I s it going to rain on this very special night?
V erses of songs are learnt off by heart
A ll the crowds are smiling all night
L ast of the floats is riding past me,
    now this is the end of a wonderful night.

Ilkay Kolcak
Sedgemoor Manor Junior School

ANIMALS

A bird that tweets is so sweet
A lion that roars knocks down doors
Giraffes are tall, even taller than a hall
Rhinos are nasty and they hate pasties
Hippos are fat unlike a bat
Lizards hate blizzards
Kangaroos hate the zoo.

Liam Riddle (8)
Sedgemoor Manor Junior School

I KNOW WHAT THE BOYS ARE UP TO!

The boys are in the backyard
Playing cards
They're having fun
Eating an iced bun

Yum, yum, yum!
I'm not dumb.
They're always nasty
When I eat a pasty.

Samantha Webber (10)
Sedgemoor Manor Junior School

OUR TEACHER SINGS!

When Miss goes 'Laaa!' we go 'Ahhh!'

If she sings, she will kill a king!

If she dances, she breaks some glasses!

Because that's what our silly teacher is like!

Ben Ward   (10)
Sedgemoor Manor Junior School

I WISH, I WISH

I wish I had a dog, that was scared of fog,
I wish I had a cat, that was ugly and fat,
I wish I had a fish, that swam in a dish,
I wish I had a rat, that wore a woolly hat,
I wish I had a mouse that could lift up a house,
I wish I had a bee, that could drink a cup of tea,
I wish I had a bear, that could wear my underwear.

That's all I want for me.

Joanna Hall (9)
Sedgemoor Manor Junior School

SEASICK

As I stepped on the boat, the water went splish, splash, splosh.
I entered the boat and the Captain said 'Get out your dosh.'
Vroom, vroom, vroom went the engine as we left the bay.
The boat did swing and sway
As the boat stopped, it did also rock
And was sick with a splish, splash, splosh.
In the water the fish came to the top,
With a flip, flap, flop, to see what was up.

Tanya Hughes (9)
Sedgemoor Manor Junior School

THE SUN

I am boiling hot with fire.
I live in the sky from a thousand feet high.
I have never died from being a thousand feet high in the sky.
I turn around 24 seven in the sky from a thousand feet high
I am very happy when I am hot from a thousand feet high in the sky.
I am very sad when the rain passes by from a thousand feet high
in the sky.

Hannah Cobbin (11)
Sedgemoor Manor Junior School

MY NEWTS

I love my newts, they are so cute,
They are like a frog and a lizard,
They are black and orange
And very slimy,
And when they're hungry they bite us!

Krystal Brennan (11)
Sedgemoor Manor Junior School

ONOMATOPOEIA POEM

The bath water went, splash, splosh, splash.
The cat went miaow, miaow.
The thunder went bang, bang.
My Coco Pops went snap, crackle, pop.
The floorboards went creak, creak.
The wind went swish, swosh.
The mud went slosh, slish.

Shavana Ball (10)
Sedgemoor Manor Junior School

WEATHER

The wind whistling through your hair.
The rain pitter-pattering on the back door.
The lightning crashing down the trees.
The thunder roaring in the black night.
The sun glowing in the sky.
The freezing snow on the winter's night.

Lloyd Hooper (7)
Sedgemoor Manor Junior School

CLOUDS

The clouds are like pieces of white chalk spread across blue papers,
The clouds are like white clothes in a blue washing machine,
The clouds are like white candyfloss,
The clouds are like ice cubes in glittering blue water,
The clouds are like white balls floating across the sky,
The clouds are a beautiful piece of nature.

Lauren Griffiths (10)
Sedgemoor Manor Junior School

MIRANDA, THE PANDA

My name is Miranda
and I am a panda
I sit in the zoo
having a munch and a chew
on a piece of bamboo
people say that it looks like
I have been in a fight
but I haven't, it's just the
patches around my eyes.

Jade Smith (10)
Sedgemoor Manor Junior School

BIRTHDAYS

On your birthday you grow a year older
Why a year older?
A birthday is a very special time of year
Because you grow a year older
Why a year older?

Sadie Trent (9)
Sedgemoor Manor Junior School

BATS

Bats like to hang upside down.
They live in caves.
Bats hate people coming into their caves.
They have babies.

Jenny Rowe (8)
Sedgemoor Manor Junior School

WHAT I LIKE

I like the smell of
I like the smell of hot crusty bread
hot eggs sizzling in the pan
shampoo bubbling in my hair
and gold cold perfume.

I like the sound of
I like the sound of
rain dripping on the window
water dripping down my throat
tigers roaring in the zoo
and my mum singing in the burning bath.

I like the taste of
I like the taste of watery spaghetti Bolognese
burning hot McDonald's
and smelly, tasty chips.

I like the feel of
I like the feel of my big cuddly teddy with sharp claws
shiny, glittery hair
my big purple fluffy
Soft silvery cushions.

I like the sight of
I like the sight of my mum coming back softly from the shop
My dog running through the park quickly
Fast cars zooming down the street.

Jade Gillard (7)
Sedgemoor Manor Junior School

MY PET

My pet likes to eat
a little, little treat,
my pet is quite furry.

My cat likes to drink a lot
so he can think,
my pet is so cuddly.

My pet is the best
in the kitchen he messed
so he's the best one of all.

Becky Hopper (8)
Sedgemoor Manor Junior School

MY PET

My pet is the best
but when it comes to the vets
he's a right little tarry.

My pet likes to drink
so he can think, think and think
I adore my pet.

Carla Lambert (9)
Sedgemoor Manor Junior School

DEEP IN THE FOREST

One dark night in a deep, dark village,
Stood an abandoned house.
A mysteriously blurred thing came riding by.
The red-eyed horse was going through the forest.

There was a glow behind a tree,
It was greeny-blue.
It might have been a phantom,
No one knows.

Rachel Fry (8)
Sedgemoor Manor Junior School

CROCODILE

I am a big and powerful crocodile.
I always eat people for lunch.
I am huge, like a great beast.
I jump out of the water and grab the beast.
My teeth are just like needles.
When a person goes near the water
I jump out and I will grab that person.
When it is raining I go underwater.
I will dig underwater.

Jordan Hosey (9)
Sedgemoor Manor Junior School

TEACHERS

Teachers are friendly
Teachers are scary
Teachers are stupid
Teachers are nice
Teachers are horrible
Teachers are brilliant
Teachers are bad
Teachers are excellent
Teachers are funny.

Holly Keirle (10)
Sedgemoor Manor Junior School

ONE DARK NIGHT

One dim and busy night
An enormous street, crowded with thousands of people
Waiting for midnight, to get into
The biggest shop in the world,
To go night shopping.

Suddenly a girl slipped over by a swinging door,
It was raining like breaking glass.
A man called Peter ran over to the phone box
And called an ambulance.

The ambulance came at the speed of light
And picked up the headless person and rushed to hospital.

Two fascinating men were arguing face to face
And starting to have a big fight.
The police zoomed past the shop and
Saw the fascinating men fight.

It became really dark and windy,
The lights were turned off and the big tree was swinging about.
It looked like it had a big, angry mouth,
Two dark eyes with a pointed nose.

Everyone was pretty scared and ran home.

The biggest shop in the world opened
And turned all the lights on.
A headless man saw no one there
And slammed the door shut!

Luke Hardwell (9)
Sedgemoor Manor Junior School

MONDAY TO FRIDAY

Monday

Monday is the start of the week
I wish it wasn't school.
I kick a ball and look like a fool.

Tuesday

Tuesday is a boring day,
I wish it wasn't school.
When I come home,
I pick up the phone
And chat for the rest of the day.

Wednesday

Wednesday is the worst day,
I wish it wasn't school.
I get up in a strop and watch the clock,
I get told off for making my chair rock.

Thursday
Thursday is a better day, I know,
The weekend's coming.
I sit on my desk
And have a rest.

Friday

Friday is the best day I know,
The weekend is here.
After school I run down the mall.

Kirstin White (10)
Sedgemoor Manor Junior School

MY DOG

My dog is as fast as a whirlwind,
My dog is as quick as lightning,
My dog is good at fetching sticks.

My dog has big, brown, softy eyes,
My dog is my special prize,
My dog loves me.

My dog whines when I'm not there,
My dog thinks I don't care,
But I love my dog.

Cassandra Gillard (10)
Sedgemoor Manor Junior School

THE LION IN THE LION'S DEN

The lion in the lion's den,
Would you go there?
Would you dare?
The lion in the lion's den,
Would you go there?
You will get a scare!
The lion in the lion's den,
He's fierce and lets out a roar,
The lion in the lion's den,
Run home quick and shut the door.

Jemma Tomlinson (9)
Sedgemoor Manor Junior School

FOOTBALL

Football is a lovely time
When you are a star at it like me.
Then you try some great things.
In the ball is slime.

I like football. It's fun.
Football is great fun for me.
Football
Football, it's so much fun
You go so fast when you run.

Cameron Taylor (8)
Sedgemoor Manor Junior School

FOOTBALL

F   antastic
O   n the pitch
O   f course you'll get a bit muddy
T   hings get a bit soggy
B   ut you will slip over quite a lot
A   nd show yourself up
L   ike things in the air and
L   ots of people laugh at you.

Ben Patrick (10)
Sedgemoor Manor Junior School

SHOWER

I get out of bed.
I go to the shower.
It goes *ssss!*
I get out with a thump.
I go outside.
I hear a bee buzzing.
It starts to rain, bang, bang, on the roof.
Birds go tweet, tweet,
Doors slam, balls bounce
Bells go ding, ding, it's time to go in.
At the end of the day we shout 'Yes.'
Cops come racing down the roads.

Reece Galloway (10)
Sedgemoor Manor Junior School

PETS

I had a cat and its name was Jess
It was painting pictures and she made a mess
She was asking a question and had a guess
She had a friend called Bess
She had a very, very, very good guess
Her mum was called Fay
Her dad was called Ray
Her sister was called May
Her brother was called Ray
Her other sister was called Fay.

Sophie Dilbo (9)
Sedgemoor Manor Junior School

FOOTBALL

F   unky football
O   ff the tele
O   ffside players
T   end to get angry
B   ecause the other team gets
A   free kick
L   et's cheer them on in the
L   eague Cup.

     Newcastle, Leeds, Spurs, Man United
     Liverpool, Blackburn, Chelsea, Arsenal
     Which one do you support?

Scott James (10)
Sedgemoor Manor Junior School

BEING ROSEMARY

R   is for Responsibility,
O   is for Optimistic,
S   is for Smiling,
E   is for Entertaining,
M   is for Manic,
A   is for Active,
R   is for Respectful,
Y   is for Young.

Rosemary means 'dew of the sea.'

Rosemary Ingram (11)
Sedgemoor Manor Junior School

BLUE

I like dogs, do you?
And she is the colour blue.
And I like walking her
and she is true
and she barks when she sees
the colour blue.

I like dogs, do you?
And she is the colour yellow
and I like walking her
and she's pale.

Sophie Withers (8)
Sedgemoor Manor Junior School

DOWN IN THE TOWN

One gloomy Thursday night,
It is not very shiny.
All the lights were on,
It is very scary and no one is out.

A very scary, creepy church
Is very dull and not bright,
All the kids are scared.
'Is there a ghost out there?' they say,
They leave it there . . .

Kim Dibble (8)
Sedgemoor Manor Junior School

APPLES

One, two, three, four,
Picking apples by the door
Five, six, seven, eight
Throw them over the garden gate
Nine, ten, eleven, twelve
Put them on the kitchen shelf
Thirteen, fourteen, fifteen, sixteen,
Store them in the kitchen
Seventeen, eighteen, nineteen, twenty
Eaten all the apples, my plate's empty.

Natasha Puddy (7)
Sedgemoor Manor Junior School

MONKEY

Oh, oh, oh,
Monkey, monkey, monkey.
Scratch, scratch, scratch,
Monkey, monkey, monkey,
Eat, eat, eat,
Monkey, monkey, monkey,
Crunch, crunch, crunch,
Monkey, monkey, monkey.
Out that tree . . .
               now!

Chloé Bowen (8)
Sedgemoor Manor Junior School

THE MOUSE IN THE HOUSE

Our cat Spot likes to catch us presents
From dead birds to live mice!
This is where the story begins

One day Spot came in and a tail was moving in his mouth
It swayed like a pendulum in a grandfather clock
Tick-tock, tick-tock, tick-tock
Our hearts were beating in time with the tail
Thump, thump, thump
'It's got to be his tongue doing that,' we said in hope
Ahhhhhhhhhhh! It's alive!

Brave Mum jumped onto the nearest chair
Little sister asked 'Where is the cute little mouse, where?'
It ran up in front of her
She screamed and up the stairs she ran
The mouse turned round and charged at me
In fright, I jumped onto the settee.

We tried for days to catch the beast in a little tub
Things happened to scare it back into its hiding place
A dog barked, the phone rang, the washing machine span
In desperate frustration Mum kicked the tub
It rolled across the room . . .
Out ran the mouse . . .

It crashed into the tub and it fell on him
Hooray, hooray! The mouse was caught,
One more problem . . .
How do we get the mouse out of the tub? Out of the house?
That was for Dad to figure out!

Jade Stone (10)
Sedgemoor Manor Junior School

FRIENDS

F   is for friends working together.
R   is for realising that we are friends.
I   is for giving ideas to your friends.
E   is for when people end up being friends
N   is for not being nasty to your friends.
D   is for Dad when he says, 'Come in,' to your friends.
S   is for sharing things with your friends.

Miles Beacham (10)
Sedgemoor Manor Junior School

WHAT IS . . . THE SUN?

The sun is a yellow lemon
Sitting in a fruit bowl

It is the centre of an egg
Cracked in a saucepan

It is a golden coin falling
Into the blue water of
A wishing well.

It is a yellow clock without
The hands.

It is a hot air balloon sailing
Through the summer sky

It is an orb floating in the air

It is a red top of a milk bottle

Richard Townsend (11)
West Coker Primary School

HORROR MEAL

First Course

Start simmering five empty eye sockets added to three screams
of horror.
Whisk three hairy spiders, then dice finely.
Add half a dozen noisy floors then slowly squeeze in three chopped
frogs' legs.

Main Course

Bake four pints of blood and leave to cool.
Smoke two narrow ravens and put one clap of thunder on top, then cook
for 30 minutes.
Boil a packet of rustling leaves and sprinkle over four screeching birds.

Dessert

Put three things that go bump in the night and put in shadows
on the walls.
Mix two howling winds and sauté one flash of lightning.

Now your dish is finished.

Gemma Louise Bowditch (10)
West Coker Primary School

WHAT IS THE SKY?

The sky is a blue waterfall going into a stream.
It is a blue ring, on my finger.
It is a wave, floating in the water.
It is wind, coming from the west, and
It is a blue dolphin, playing in the water.

Gemma Powell (9)
West Coker Primary School

WHAT IS A . . . RAINBOW?

A rainbow . . .

It is a splash of food colouring on a yellow cake.

It is a scarf on an orange washing line.

It is where a baby flicked some paint on an indigo wall.

It is a row of children in a blue swimming pool wearing
different-coloured costumes.

It is a packet of fruit pastilles bought from Violet's shop.

It is a multicoloured pencil case on an arc-shaped desk.

It is Christmas lights on a dark green fir tree.

It is school bags scattered on a rainy day.

It is tops spread in a shop window.

It is a swirl of colours when you're dizzy, floating across a dark red sky.

Amy Harriss (11) & Holly Dover (11)
West Coker Primary School

THE BEACH

The beach is a curved banana
Resting on a blue piece of paper,
And its waves eat at the fruit
With their yellowy, pointy teeth,
Seaweed hanging like a fringe of hair
Along the sea floor,
Is brushed away by the tide.

Adam Beckey (10)
West Coker Primary School

WHAT IS . . . THE WORLD?

The world is a huge football,
Painted blue and green.

It is a round sphere,
Turning around in space.

It is the top of a bottle,
Lying on black paper.

It is a spinning top,
Whirling in the air.

It is a balloon,
Floating in the black sky.

Sherrie Dampier (10) & Emma Simpson (11)
West Coker Primary School

WHAT IS . . . THE MOON?

The moon is a hot air balloon,
    Floating in the sky.

        The moon is a weightless ball,
        Orbiting the Earth

The moon is a clock,
Ticking in time.

The moon is a rubber,
Erasing the darkness.

Robert Curtis, Terry Sollis
        & Katherine Foster (10)
West Coker Primary School

WHAT IS ... THE SUN?

It's an orange piece of fruit
In its fruit bowl.

It's a golden coin
Dropped down the drain.

It's a red-hot balloon
Gliding through the sky.

It's a shiny lemon
On a sheet of blue paper.

It's the centre of an egg
Cracked in a saucepan.

Joshua Nutland (11)
West Coker Primary School

FIRE

Fire is a red-hot warning,
A caged animal,
Blow it out,
Like a giant candle
Dying of tears;
It is like a fierce, orange sun
Hell comes alive,
And it brings warning.

Holly Edmonds (11)
West Coker Primary School

WALKING IN THE WIND

Walking slowly in the street
Arms up high
Hats on low
Warm woollen mittens on our hands
Walking to the park with Katie, the best
I feel cold
The wind's so strong
Leaves all blustering all along the road
My eyes are so cold from the stinging wind
Long white feathers falling from the sky
Falling on the ground, trying to make me cry
Trees on the way, trying to blow away,
Telephone wires tangled in the wind,
Telephones not working, mobiles are.
Hope I'm nearly home,
'Oh yes I am'
Round the corner and here I am.
Glad I'm home inside the house with
Mum, Dad, and baby brother, Ben.
It's nippy outside
Thunder and lightning,
Streaks and sparks
Leaves are flying around outside,
Helicopters crash, so do planes
Buildings fall down
Because of the wild wind
The wild wind
Foggy/icy/Arctic strong all day
Blizzards and streaks
Blizzards and streaks
Trees are swaying, battered and twisty.

I'm glad I'm still home.

Katherine Foster (10)
West Coker Primary School

WHAT IS . . . THE MOON?

The moon is a silver balloon
Floating in the dark sky
It is a shiny yellow banana
Lying on a black worktop
It is a grey globe sitting
All alone in a dark room.

Earle Neville (10)
West Coker Primary School

LION

Stalking, crouching, tracking down,
Leaping, jumping, round and round.
My fluffy orange coat, my mane dangling around,
Great hunk of meat that I have found.

Walking through the jungle, feeling proud,
King of the jungle, roaring loud.
Little black whiskers, long swishy tail,
Middle-sized head, white and pale.

Slowly I prowl,
As I see my prey I growl.
I pounce, I devour,
I live forever.

Vicky Moore (10)
Woolavington Village Primary School

BELLA

Head between paws
Eyes darting at any sound
But still she hears nothing
Until . . .

Footsteps walking on the gravel

Suddenly her head jerks
She scents the air

Eyes peering through the window

She sees a man
With a black suit.

Her lips tremble

A low growl

She snarls

I am safe.

Carrianne Smith (10)
Woolavington Village Primary School

MY CAT BEES

My cat's name is Beesybumble,
He smells like a bar of soap,
That's my Beesybumble,
My grandma calls him Beesybundle,
But that's not his name,
My mum says that he's her little baby,
That's my Beesybumble.

Holly Cox (9)
Woolavington Village Primary School

RED

Two fully grown poppies squashed in the field.
A sparkling bright bottle lid in the classroom.
Lots of pippy dark red grapes in a plastic box.
A bright red marker pen glowing in the sun.
A red balloon bobbing in the air.
A red sticker stuck on the wardrobe.
Lots of brightly-coloured RE books.

Deborah Hirst (8)
Woolavington Village Primary School

YELLOW

The melon hanging on the tree all juicy and sweet
The glittering gold hidden underneath the hard ground
The bright sun shining fresh and gold on the desert
The chicks cheep as they swim in the pond
The waving daffodils on a hill all covered in the hillside
The hot sand all bumpy with big shells all shapes and sizes.

Liam Whatley (8)
Woolavington Village Primary School

BLUE

At the beautiful beach the shimmering shining sea lay on the gold sand.
The huge whale passed a simmering fish in the shining sea.
An Egyptian bug bit a person, it really hurt
The silky yellow fabric with dark blue small stars were brighter
than ever.

Ben Hiley (8)
Woolavington Village Primary School

RED

Juicy cherries on a tree
Roses dancing around
Colour of blood
Calls for danger
Dangerous fire
Sparkly paint.

Iona Neilson (8)
Woolavington Village Primary School

WINTER

Whistling winds passing through the trees; leaves
                          settling on the ground.
Squirrels jumping from tree to tree.
Birds sleeping in their nests.

Michael Moares (8)
Woolavington Village Primary School

RED

The beautiful red robin flies around
Tomatoes squirt seeds from their skin
Poppies are blowing around in different directions
Spotty ladybirds making colonies in rows.

Honey Halliday (8)
Woolavington Village Primary School

BORDER TERRIER

Tail wagging faster than a bird's flapping wings,
Small, creased ears stand to attention when called,
Catch me if you can!
I'm a tail-chaser!

Prickly whiskers twitching in sleep,
Licking his razor-sharp teeth with a rough, pink tongue,
Small, shiny nose,
Sniffing at the morning air.

Trotting through the long, green grass,
Dewdrops soaking small padded paws,
Eyes drawn towards the burning sun,
Is my little Border terrier.

Holly Jago (11)
Woolavington Village Primary School

DOLPHINS

Dolphins swim like a fish
they're elegant and graceful and everything nice
there's bottlenose, normal and spinner dolphins
with a spotted in-between.

Dolphins, dolphins, squeak and squawk
they jump like a kangaroo
and twist like a snake
I like you, dolphins.

Tiffany Boobyer (9)
Woolavington Village Primary School

MY RABBIT BUGGSY

My rabbit is called Buggsy
She has got a huge hutch
But she has spoilt it by being buggsy
And biting it so much.

Buggsy won't hurt a fly
But she has bitten me once
She likes eating pies.

Buggsy is really fluffy
All the fluff gets in my face
And we were going to call her Duffy.

Joanne Marsh (8)
Woolavington Village Primary School

ANIMALS

Animals are friendly creatures
Except for tigers and lions.
The only time you don't know what's what
Is when they playing with irons.

Animals all have a sound.
The horse is the best,
They neigh and neigh and eat the hay,
Until it's time to rest.

Animals are sometimes a mess.
They mess and mess and sometimes dress,
And they just get more of a mess.

Stacy Moore (8)
Woolavington Village Primary School

FREEDOM

Freedom is
Birds high across the sky
Wind blowing over the countryside
A leaf falling to create the Earth
Fish gliding past unknown lands
Waves brewing far out at sea
Stars floating in colonies across the galaxy . . .
. . . Freedom is home . . .

Ryan Dicks (11)
Woolavington Village Primary School

TURQUOISE

The sky, the beautiful sky is covered
In glittery, bumpy, shiny clouds covering
The bright sun and round moon, day and night.
You need sunglasses to look up at the sparkling
                                    rays in the sky.

James Olive (8)
Woolavington Village Primary School

GREEK SCHOOLS

When the Greek boys go to Greek schools
Greek girls stay at Greek homes
Greek boys learn Greek work
While Greek girls stay at Greek homes
And clean up the Greek homes.

Gabrielle Roper (8)
Woolavington Village Primary School

THE GAME

Running onto the pitch
The excitement of playing another match
Cheers from the crowd roaring in my ears.

Memories of scoring a try,
Can I gain a second?
New skills each match.

The trust and friendship of the players
Making sure everyone's included
The fairness of the referee.

Plastered in mud
The whole team jumps with the thrill of winning the game.

Dominik Griffin (10)
Woolavington Village Primary School

ROMANCE

He's the topping on every dish I make,
And icing on my birthday cake,
He can always make me laugh out loud,
Always gets noticed in a crowd,
He's the lemon in a lemon tart,
He's the romance of my heart.

Hannah Halliday (10)
Woolavington Village Primary School

MY AFFENPINSCHER

I eat, I sleep,
I like being fussed,
I am a big part of the family,
And I love being brushed.

I go out for walks,
And I get pretty muddy,
It sticks to my fur,
And I chase the green budgie.

I toss, I turn,
I struggle, I flinch
And my dog breed is,
an affenpinscher.

Vikki Thomas (11)
Woolavington Village Primary School

FRIENDSHIP

Friends are loving and caring,
Happiness spreads with friends,
Joy is always round the place,
Friendship never ends.

Friends are always there,
No matter what you do,
Friendship is for life
Especially for me and you.

Amy Sparrow (10)
Woolavington Village Primary School

HAPPINESS

Happiness is:
Sun smiling on a Sussex garden,
A day out in the park with my family,
Disco dancing to the strong beat of music,
Giving and receiving thoughtful gifts,
A day off school on a rainy day watching daytime TV,
Playing with my friends in the deep snow,
Writing stories, poems and maths at school,
Chatting at a sleepover at my house,
My mum tucking me up in my bed each night,
A quiet evening at home with my family.
Happiness is a world with peace and happiness.

Cally Etherington (10)
Woolavington Village Primary School

LIVE

I'm powerful yet invisible,
At home but come to school.
I roam free,
As a worldwide resource,
Not guarded but a treasure,
I'm a jewel that's good in all weather.
Colourful yet plain,
Fun in the pouring rain,
But how is this without you?

William Newcomb (11)
Woolavington Village Primary School

DREAMS

Dreams are so peaceful,
Dreams are so good,
Laughing clowns,
Sparkling fairies,
Noisy sounds,
Tasty cheese dairies.

Big boxes of chocolates,
Dolls sitting in a room,
A garden full of rain droplets,
Marching in the light of the moon.

Yasmin Millverton-Collier (10)
Woolavington Village Primary School

CLUMSY FOREST

Way up high in a banana tree,
A tiger stepped on a chimpanzee,
The chimpanzee with tears in
His eyes said
'Pick on someone your own size.'

Right down low on the forest floor,
A crocodile stepped on a tiger's paw,
The tiger said with a great big roar,
'Now you've made my foot sore.'

Richard Stewart (9)
Woolavington Village Primary School

HORSES

Touch me
Stroke me
Feel my soft fur
My brown face
My high speed
My shiny hooves
My power.

I canter
I trot
I am as fast as the wind.
My saddle
My bridle
My red numnah and girth.

I stand in my stable
Surrounded by feed and hay.
Waiting for the footsteps
Ears go forward
Here comes my rider.

Grace Dear (11)
Woolavington Village Primary School